BOSPHORUS

SEA OF MARMARA

THRACE

PANGAEUM MTS

Kavalla

Abdera

THASOS

SAMOTHRACE

Thessalonika

Stagira

MT. ATHOS

IMBROS

ASIA

TROAD

LEMNOS

HELLESPONT

Troy

MINOR

Scamander R.

MT. IDA

MT. OSSA

SALY

MT. PELION

AEGEAN

NORTHERN SPORADES

Mytilene

Pergamum

SKIATHOS

LESBOS (MYTILENE)

SCYROS

LYDIA

PHOKIS

GULF OF EUBOEA

EUBOEA

CHIOS

Sardis

Delphi

Chaeronea

BOEOTIA

AEGEAN
ISLANDS

Cayster

Ephesus

Meander R.

GULF OF CORINTH

Eleusis

Thebes

Marathon

ANDROS

SAMOS

Priene

Sicyon

Lechaion

Megara

Athens

Corinth

Cenchrea

Salamis

Piraeus

ATTICA

Laurium

TENOS

Miletus

SARONIC GULF

AEGINA

CAPE SUNIUM

RHENEIA

MYKONOS

Didyma

CARIA

ADIA

Mycenae

Argos

Tiryns

Troezen

DELOS

Halicarnassus

Hermione

CYCLADES

SERIPHOS

PAROS

NAXOS

KOS

PONNESE

SIPHNOS

Sparta

AMORGOS

Rhodes

Epidaurus

MELOS

DODECANESE

RHODES

CAPE MALEA

THERA

Lindos

KYTHERA

KARPHATHOS

SEA OF CRETE

DIA

Mallia

Cydonia

Herakleion

Knossos

Palaikastro

MT. IDA

CRETE

Gournia

Zakros

Hagia Triada

Phaistos

THE ARCHAEOLOGY
OF **Greece**
AND THE
**Aegean**

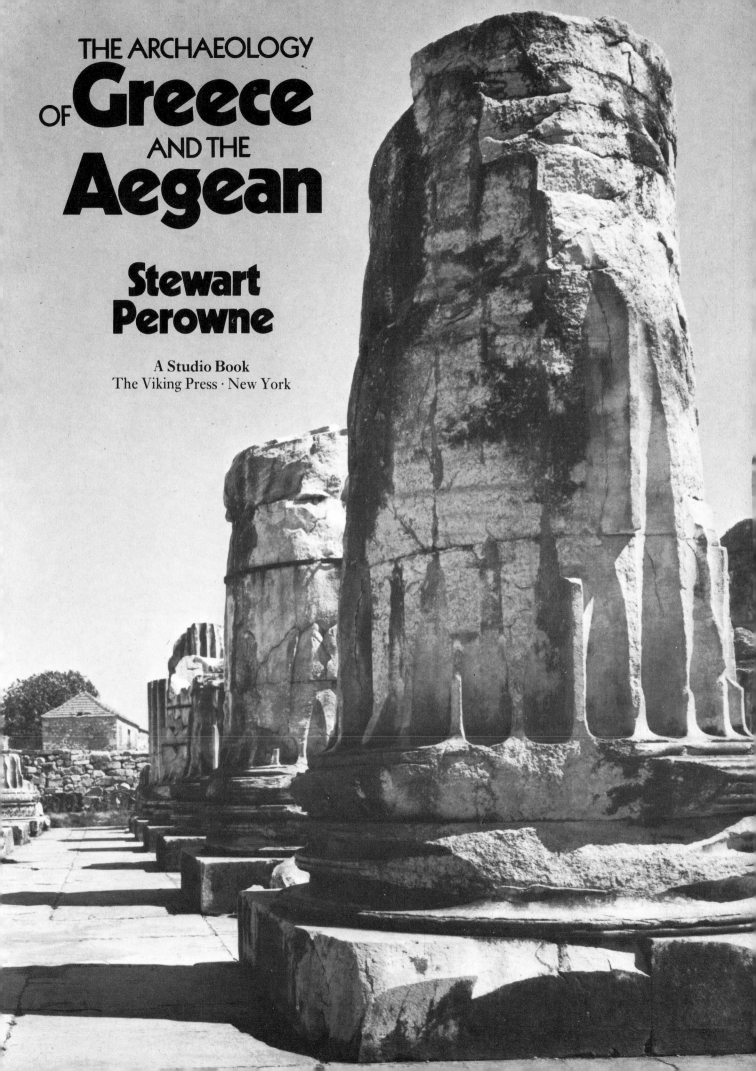

# THE ARCHAEOLOGY
## OF **Greece**
### AND THE
# Aegean

## Stewart Perowne

A Studio Book
The Viking Press · New York

# Contents

Acknowledgments

Thomas Y. Crowell Company,
Inc. and Faber & Faber Ltd:
from *Hellenic Traveller*
by Guy Pentreath.
Copyright © 1964
by Guy Pentreath.
With permission of
Thomas Y. Crowell Company,
Inc. and Faber & Faber Ltd.

Original edition published
in England by The Hamlyn
Publishing Group Limited,
Feltham, Middlesex

Copyright © 1974 the Hamlyn
Publishing Group Limited
All rights reserved

Published in 1974 by The
Viking Press, Inc.
625 Madison Avenue,
New York, NY. 10022

Published simultaneously in
Canada by The Macmillan
Company of Canada Limited

SBN 670–13050–8

Library of Congress Catalog
Card number: 73–19042

Printed in Spain by
Printer Industria Gráfica sa,
Tuset 19 Barcelona,
San Vicente dels Horts, 1974
Depósito Legal B. 26675-1974
Mohn Gordon Ltd., London

# Author's Note

Egypt's might is tumbled down,

Down a-down the deeps of thought;

Greece is fallen and Troy town,

Glorious Rome hath lost her crown,

Venice' pride is nought.


But the dreams their children dreamed,

Fleeting, unsubstantial, vain,

Shadowy as the shadows seemed,

Airy nothing, as they deemed,

These remain.


It is as a modest believer in the faith
expressed by Mary Coleridge in these lines
that I have attempted the present essay.

S.P. 1974

ACKNOWLEDGMENTS FOR ILLUSTRATIONS

*Colour*
Camera Press 17 (T), 17 (B), 20, 28 (TR), 88; Sonia Halliday 81 (T), 85; Michael Holford Library 24–25, 84 (BR); Spectrum Colour Library 29 (B), 84 (T), 89 (T), 89 (B), 93; Tony Stone Associates 96, front cover. Z.F.A. 28 (TL), 28 (B), 29 (T), 32, 81 (B), 84 (BL) 92, back cover.

The illustration at the top of page 29 is reproduced by Gracious Permission of Her Majesty the Queen.

Other BLACK & WHITE photographs were provided by the following: American School of Classical Studies, Corinth, 47; Ashmolean Museum (Department of Antiquities) 12–13; Bavaria–Verlag 7, 100, 103, 115, 126; Bildarchiv Foto Marburg 58; E. Boudot–Lamotte 40–41; Camera Press 76, 99, 135; C. M. Dixon 34–35; Arpad Elfer 51(R); Hirmer Fotoarchiv 11, 22, 26, 31, 33, 40 (TL), 41 (B), 59, 62–63, 63, 64, 68, 69, 70, 72–73, 73, 74 (B) 75, 77, 78, 87, 129 (T); Institute of Archaeology, London 10 (T); A. F. Kersting 6, 14–15, 37, 39, 83 (T), 86, 110, 129 (B), 130–131, 131 (C), 131 (B), 134, 136–137; Lauros–Giraudon 97; Edward Leigh 18, 23; Mansell–Alinari 43, 128 (T); Mansell–Alinari–Giraudon 116; Mansell–Anderson 124–125, 128 (B); Mansell Collection 9, 10 (B), 19, 27 (C), 42, 52, 53, 54–55, 60, 80, 82, 91, 106, 133; Federico Arborio Mella 38 (T), 38 (B), 48, 49, 50–51, 83 (B), 121; National Tourist Organisation of Greece 104, 112; Antonello Perissinotto title page, 117, 119, 120, 122, 123; Radio Times Hulton Picture Library 55 (T), 71; Edwin Smith 8, 44, 46, 57 (B), 109, 132 (T), 132 (B); Spectrum Colour Library 67, 74 (T), 101, 102, 104–105, 107, 118; Nick Stournaras half-title; Viewpoint Projects 30, 90, 98; H. Roger Viollet 27 (B), 56–57, 61, 62 (TL); Z.F.A. 95.

To Christopher Scaife
'A Latter Day Athenian'

# CHAPTER I
# Time's Cantilever

Both time and space have shown themselves in our day to be not only infinite but indefinable. New worlds have beckoned to mundane man, worlds so infinitely distant in space that their remoteness can only be measured in terms of time – of light-years. The mere prospect of futurity, of those vast avenues of time perpetuating themselves beyond knowledge, of not merely a world but of worlds without end, has struck terror into men's minds, but it has implanted resolution too. The future must be faced, the unknown made familiar. But we can grasp what is to come only if we hold fast to what has gone before. The great cantilever must stand firm.

That is the meaning of archaeology, and the reason why archaeology is to-day so much studied, sought after and promoted. Back, back we must go to find the counterweight of the past. We must call the old world into existence to redress the balance of the new. Thus we have in archaeology a paradoxical pleasure and comfort, because it is the aim of archaeology to tell us the newest about the oldest.

Modern archaeology has by a process of evolution gone back to what archaeology originally was when in the Aegean Sea the Greeks of Ionia set out on the unending journey. The Ionian philosophers of the seventh and sixth centuries BC were fascinated by origins: how did the universe come into existence? Of what is it formed? This really is the basic problem of all subsequent archaeology. This logical, rational approach to the destiny of man had a strong influence on poets: they were reluctant to abandon their myths, but they did realize, it seems, that there had been an age before their own which was better than theirs. The Golden Age was always in the past.

This attitude of mind and conduct is perfectly summed up by Tennyson in his *In Memoriam* published in 1850 – just when men were once more bewildered by the clash of past and present, by the apparent conflict between the Christian ethic of future felicity and the claim of so-called rationalism:

And is it that the haze of grief
   Makes former gladness loom so great?
   The lowness of the present state,
That sets the past in this relief?

Or that the past will always win
   A glory from its being far;
   And orb into the perfect star
We saw not when we moved therein?

Paganism was always pessimistic. There were, it is true, brief periods when men escaped from the tyranny of the gods. Fifth-century Athens was one. Tragedians, philosophers, rulers all held that man could move forward; and they did all in their power to help him do so. Their works still urge us in the same direction. But here as always with archaeology we must be careful not to rely on our own eyes. These men were not, they said, constructing the future, they were reforming the past. Alexander the Great was another reforming genius, who for all too short a season rescued men from despair.

This preoccupation with bygone things and ideas induced the Greeks to invent the word *archaeology*, which means simply 'talking about the old or out of date'. Thucydides and Plato both knew the word, so did Plutarch. The idea of the bygone Golden Age continued under the Roman domination. Again we find a 'pocket' of optimism. Pliny, the encyclopaedist who lost his life in the eruption of Vesuvius in AD 79, lauds the 'infinite majesty' of the Roman peace; but in the next century a Greek historian of Rome, Dio Cassius, says that the golden age ended with the philosopher-emperor Marcus Aurelius and that by his own day the affairs of Rome had descended into an age of 'iron and rust'.

Already, though, the expression 'infinite majesty' was being applied in an entirely new context. Paul of Tarsus in Cilicia, Jew, Roman citizen and Christian pioneer, had bid men turn their backs on the past, and to press on towards the goal of a Christian future. This novel view, strengthened by some very strong spirits of whom the greatest was Saint Augustine, was able to build a city not made with hands, the 'City of God'. This city remained paramount for a millenium. No archaeology was needed to explore or explain it. Then in the fifteenth century a new spirit began to move over the waters of Faith. Archaeology was back; but in a far different manifestation. It was to be the guide of a new

Lucius Cornelius Sulla, 138–78 BC, the ruthless and enigmatic Roman dictator who systematically looted Athens in 86 BC.

*Opposite*
The Via Appia, 'Queen of Roads', called after its creator the blind censor Appius Claudius, who constructed it on an existing track in 312 BC. Originally it ran south to Capua, and was later extended as far as Taranto and Brindisi. It was among the funerary monuments which still line this road that the sarcophagus was discovered, in 1485, which contained the perfectly preserved body of a Roman girl.

age. Starting as a pastime, it became an art, and then a science. The archaeology we know and practise is an amalgam of all three, which is why it enthralls and satisfies us as it does.

The new era started, like so much else, in Rome. In April 1485 workmen looking for marble – that is, looting ancient structures – on the Appian Way, unearthed a marble sarcophagus in which lay a perfectly preserved mummy of a Roman beauty of imperial days. The body, exhibited in the Palazzo dei Conservatori two days later attracted a crowd of twenty-thousand a day. Pope Innocent VIII ordered the body to be buried at night outside the Porta Pinciana. All we now possess is one sketch done at the time. The interest excited by this find naturally distressed the Pope: naked women, even ancient ones, were not yet in fashion; but the find and the excitement it caused were symptomatic not only of a reviving sexual freedom but also of a reviving interest in antiquity. 'Now,' writes a modern scholar, 'in this age of rebirth of interest in classical antiquity, people were learning to think, feel, and to create anew in its spirit, though they sometimes misunderstood it. A wonder-struck populace stood ready to imbibe the very breath of remote times. Their excitement suggests that something new was truly in the air.' The past of which the Roman maiden was ambassadress had come to light again and was to rebuild the culture of the West.

Archaeology was about to dawn: its harbingers had already appeared. In 1119 and 1162 papal decrees had protected the columns of Trajan and Marcus Aurelius in Rome. They still stand. In mid-twelfth century, a bishop of Winchester had acquired classical statues and sent them to England. In 1337 Petrarch, a Florentine, paid his first visit to Rome. He was there again in 1341, to be crowned as Laureate on the Capitol. He travelled widely, in France, Germany and Flanders, searching diligently for manuscripts for his library. His collection became so important that the Republic of Venice bestowed a palace on Petrarch on condition that he leave his library to the Republic. In Liege he found two new orations of Cicero, in Verona a collection of Cicero's letters, in Florence an unknown work of Quintilian. Petrarch was the earliest of the great humanists of the Renaissance and was the true founder of modern classical culture. He died in 1374.

Some thirty years later the great Florentine architect Brunelleschi organized the first excavations in Rome. He is suspected of treasure-hunting. This form of covetousness has been the bane of archaeology for centuries and still is. It was a Roman who began it. Sulla, a cruel and rapacious dictator, captured Athens in 86 BC, and then systematically looted both it and Piraeus. Gold, silver, bullion, plate as much as he could lay hands on were sent back to Rome to adorn his triumph. With them went large quantities of paintings, statues, inscriptions, even marble columns and architectural ornaments from buildings, including the bronze cornice from the arsenal at Piraeus. Pillars from the unfinished Olympieium were requisitioned to help rebuild the temple of Jupiter on the Capitol. Not everything reached Rome. One ship is known to have been sunk

off Cape Malea. Another went down off the coast of Tunisia, having been blown off course in a gale such as wrecked St Paul in neighbouring Malta. It had no less than sixty marble columns on board, which were no doubt responsible for the ship's foundering. The columns still lie on the sea-bed, but several works in bronze and marble were salvaged and now grace the Bardo Museum. In 1959 during street-repairs in Piraeus, there came to light several exquisite bronze statues. They were quite near the surface, and lay in what appears to be the charred remains of a warehouse. The inference is that they were part of Sulla's loot, awaiting shipment to Rome. They are now prize exhibits in the National Museum at Athens.

Greek art soon became the fashion in Rome. Cicero was an amateur; but Cicero paid for what he acquired. Others were not so nice. The lords of Rome not infrequently helped themselves. The emperor Constantine reversed the process when he ordered that as many leading examples as possible of Greek sculpture be sent to embellish his new city, his new Rome, on the Bosphorous. It was thus that that famous bronze horses of Venice, originally Greek steeds attached to a Roman quadriga, found their way to Byzantium, whence they were once again looted by the most disgraceful of all recorded

Francesco Petrarca (Petrarch), 1304–74. The Italian poet and humanist who has been called the true founder of modern classical culture. Portrait by G. Bellini in the Capitoline Museum, Rome.

are now rare. The reason is that during the Middle Ages bronze artifacts continued to be in high demand; and that bronze will melt at about 1000°C, or two-thirds of the heat required for the less comely iron. Men therefore flung into the melting-pot any 'processed' bronze that came along–statues, or vessels, or even (most destructively) the bronze dowels they were able to dig from the column-drums or walls of ancient buildings, many of which were wrecked in this way.

The Venice horses found sanctuary in a church. The unique equestrian statue of Marcus Aurelius on the Capitol – the model for so many later ones – is there because he was mistaken for Constantine, the first Christian emperor.

Poggio was too pessimistic. There was far more treasure available than he supposed; and the process of identifying, classifying and assembling it, that is archaeology as we understand it, had already begun. In the year 1391 was born the remarkable man generally known as Cyriacus of Ancona. His father was a merchant called Philippo Pizzicolli, a name which his classical-minded son modulated into 'Picenicolles, o de Piceni Collibus'. (St Cyriac was the patron saint of Ancona.) At the age of nine he began to accompany his elders on mercantile trips round Italy. He did this for four years. After staying at home for the next eight, he determined to see more of the world; and during the years 1412–1414 he visited Egypt, the Aegean, Sicily and Dalmatia. In 1418 he is in Constantinople, and three years later meets his patron Cardinal Condulmier, later to become Pope. Cyriac was now a dedicated traveller. After Venice in 1423, he paid his first visit to Rome as an archaeologist. By way of a prolonged peregrination of the Levant, he revisits Rome in 1435. Illyria, Epirus and Greece all drew him, and in September 1436 he again contemplates the Pyramids. In the next year he becomes the first explorer of the Peloponnese, which at that time, after two centuries

*Above*
Drawings by Jacques Carrey of the pediments of the Parthenon as they appeared in 1674. The top two drawings are of the east pediment, the lower two of the west.

*Right*
Antonio Canova, 1757–1822, the last great 'classic' sculptor. A man of great charm and tact, he was sent to Paris in 1815 to negotiate the return to Italy of Napoleon's thefts. In 1803 he saw the Elgin Marbles in Rome on their way to England. He said, when asked to 'restore' them, that they were 'the work of the ablest artists the world has ever seen and it would be a sacrilege for me or any man to presume to touch them with a chisel'.

'archaeological' devastations, the sack of Constantinople by the Fourth Crusade in 1204. One has only to visit the cathedral of St Mark in Venice to realize what an immense storehouse of beauty, of precious metals, crystals and enamels, was at that time dissipated or destroyed. This form of rapine has continued down to our own day, and has been aggravated, in Italy especially, by the invention of the mechanical plough, because this useful machine has probed strata that had been hidden for millenia. The *clandestini* have reaped their harvest. As late as April 1973, the Italian press reported that in a newly-identified Etruscan necropolis near Grosseto, the *clandestini* had already robbed more than 120 tombs. On the other hand it was this same plough that legitimately enriched the British Museum with two of the finest treasures ever unearthed, those of Sutton Hoo (1939), and Mildenhall (1942).

In the middle of the fifteenth century, Poggio Bracciolini laments that less than a dozen of the sculptures of ancient Rome are left. Fourth-century Rome is recorded to have possessed 3,785 bronze statues, 22 equestrian statues, 53 gold and ivory images of gods, and 80 gilded ones. Ancient bronzes

of rivalry between Frankish barons and Byzantine overlords, was already tributary to the Ottomans. In 1447 he set out on his last voyage which again took him to the Peloponnese. He died in 1452.

This indefatigable enthusiast had collected antiquities wherever he went. There was little method of his proceedings: he had the jackdaw instinct for acquiring anything that shone. He described his collections in six volumes of notes. These were all lost in 1514. But his work, and most important of all his enthusiasm, endured. From 1431 to 1447 Cyriac's friend and patron had reigned as Pope Eugenius IV.

It is not surprising, therefore, to learn that in 1471 the then reigning pontiff Sixtus IV set about collecting ancient statuary in Rome. His example was followed by other prelates and princes.

It is against this background of awakening interest in the past and its glories that we must set the discovery of the sarcophagus on the Appian Way. Collectors have generally in the nature of things been rich; even where the discovery of treasure has been fortuitous; but the idea that it is only the rich amateurs who appreciate what is found is quite wrong. How widespread and general is interest in

The Laocoön, the marble group found in 1506 by De Fredi in the ruins of Nero's Golden House in Rome. It is the work of Agesander of Rhodes and his sons Athenodorus and Polidorus (1st or 2nd century BC).

The Parian stone, now in the Ashmolean Museum, Oxford. It contains, in just discernible characters, an epitome of Greek history from the reign of Kekrops, 1450 BC, to the archonship of Diotimus, 354 BC.

archaeology was proved to the point of bewilderment by the patient crowds who waited outside the British Museum in 1972 to catch even a hurried sight of the wonders of the tomb of Tutankhamun.

So far, archaeology has been, at its worst, dowsing for treasure; at its best, the search for manuscripts and inscriptions. That is, the archaeologist's approach to antiquity had been literary, as it often still very properly is. The discovery of a new text, the decipherment of another script – these are still hailed as archaeological victories. But in 1506 occurred an event which was to link archaeology and art in a union which has lasted ever since, by no means always with the happiest results. The event which makes 1506 a turning point in the history of aesthetics was the discovery, near the basilica of Santa Maria Maggiore, of the famous Laocoön. When Michelangelo saw it, he was with the sculptor Francesco da Sangallo, who at once recognized the group as being the 'Laocoön mentioned by Pliny'. The meeting has a double interest; first because it unites the literary with the actual, and secondly because it tells us of Michelangelo confronted for the first time with a work of art which was to have a profound influence on the sculptors of the Renaissance. According to Pliny, the group was created in the first century BC by a Rhodian sculptor, Agesander, and his two sons. It shews Lacoön, the priest who warned the Trojans against the Wooden Horse, with his sons, wrestling with two sea-serpents who are about to strangle him.

The profound influence which this one chance discovery had upon art, specially sculpture, was to last for three whole centuries, long after finer examples of Greek genius, examples of a very different tendency, had been discovered. Like the Laocoön, many of these later-found sculptures came from the soil of Italy, notably from Rome itself and from Herculaneum, a recompense, even when effected by looting, for the Roman looting of Greece. Such was Laocoön's hold on the taste of Europe that art was largely strangled by it. The most

remarkable testimony to the staying-power of this single work is that of Canova, the last great 'classic' sculptor. Canova was one of the commission sent to Paris in 1815 to recover the works of art which Napoleon had stolen from Italy. These included the Venice horses, which had been filched for the third, or possibly fourth, time, the Belvedere Apollo, and the Laocoön. In writing to a friend Canova said that he was now the guardian of the two greatest productions of Greek sculpture, meaning the Apollo and the Laocoön. The Laocoön had been restored (wrongly as it turned out, when another version came to light in the twentieth century); but it was Canova who had defied convention when he set eyes on the Elgin marbles. They were, he said, surpassingly and uniquely beautiful, would that he had his working life over again. He refused to touch them. John Flaxman made the same refusal.

Until that epoch very few lovers of the arts had even seen the Acropolis of Athens, although by Canova's time large collections of Greek and Roman antiquities had been formed in almost every country of Europe, and in England itself.

The favourites of King James I had been keen collectors. Thomas Howard, Earl of Arundel and George Villiers, Duke of Buckingham were eager rivals, and each contrived to amass a number of treasures. The Arundel marbles were dissipated by his boorish grandson; some lost, others destroyed. One of the most important, the 'Parian stone' which contains an epitome of Greek history through a period of 1,318 years, was broken, and the upper half of it was found built into a chimney of Arundel House, much to the justified indignation of the French who had failed to obtain it. Of the original 250 inscribed marbles 136, including the Parian Stone, went to Oxford where they still remain. The British ambassador in Constantinople, Sir Thomas Roe, acted as agent both for Buckingham and for Arundel. On one occasion he wrote to Buckingham: 'I have found that there are many antiquities in marble on the Island of Delos which I can take without trouble or prohibition, whatsoever his Grace pleases.' Even Asia Minor was placed under tribute by Roe; but Buckingham was assassinated before his final shipment arrived. Part of it appears to have been acquired by the hated Arundel, and the rest sold at auction by the regicides together with the priceless collections of the martyred King Charles.

By the middle of the seventeenth century interest in Greece and things Greek was widely diffused throughout Europe. In 1630 Louis XIII's ambassador to the Sublime Porte visited Athens. In 1645 the Jesuits settled there, to be succeeded by the French Capuchins in 1658. In 1670 they drew the first plan of Athens. This shews the Acropolis with a minaret (the Parthenon was now a mosque), and a small circular town to the north-east. The city of Perikles was now a mere township of less than ten thousand souls; but as Joannes Travlos has demonstrated in his invaluable *Poleodomike Exelixis ton Athenon* (1960) the occupied area was greater under the Turks than it had been under the Franks. Churches generally were not molested, although in 1660 the so-called Theseum was only saved from demolition by a firman from the Sultan himself. The Propylaea had been made into a fort, the intervals between the columns being filled with rude masonry. The damage to the Propylaea from which it still so visibly suffers was due to an explosion, c. 1645, of the gunpowder which was stored in the fort. The greater part of the Olympieium disappeared very early, mostly into the lime-kiln.

In 1674 Louis XIV's ambassador visited Athens, taking with him a painter called Jacques Carrey. Carrey made 400 sketches of the sculptures of the Parthenon, the two pediments, a large part of the frieze and many of the metopes. These sketches are priceless. They are preserved in the Bibliothèque Nationale.

Two years later, in 1676, a far more accurate and informative plan was drawn up by Jacques Spon, a French doctor from Lyons, and another by George Wheler, an Englishman of versatile talent who was later both ordained priest and knighted. The two companions travelled extensively in Dalmatia,

The temple of Zeus Olympios (the Olympieium), with the Akropolis in the background. It was begun by Peisistratos, mid-sixth century BC, and advanced by the Seleucid, Antiochus Epiphanes in 175 BC to the design of a Roman architect, Cossutius. The emperor Hadrian completed it in AD 131–2. Of the original 104 columns only fifteen remain erect.

Greece, and Turkey, and both wrote accounts of their voyage. Spon's is more precise, and his plans and illustrations far more accurate. Wheler's, which appeared later, and is evidently much indebted to Spon, is less antiquarian and more chatty.

Spon's plan of the city is taken from the south. It, too, shows the minareted Acropolis, with Parthenon complete and wholly roofed. Beyond, on the north side, is a mitre-shaped, enclosed town, with the various monuments and churches indicated by figures, to which a key is furnished. The 'Theseum' and most of the Agora are well outside the enceinte. On the other side the buildings stop short where Syntagma is now, with Hadrian's Arch outside, and the Choragic monument inside, what appears to be a continuous wall. This is puzzling, because Wheler says the town stretched about half a league into the plain, and was two leagues in circuit, including the Acropolis; but that it had no continuous wall. He does say, though, that the gates had been repaired and the houses on the periphery joined together as a refuge against pirates, who constantly raided the city and suburbs; so probably that is what Spon intended to represent.

Wheler also tells us that there were few ancient cities – and he saw many – so well preserved as Athens, and that the Athenians enjoyed special privileges – in theory, that is: they were constantly being overreached by greedy Turks. There were about eight to ten thousand inhabitants, of which three quarters were Greeks and the remainder Turks. There were no Jews. The Christians managed their own affairs. The city in general was under the protection and patronage, at Constantinople, of the Kislar Agha, or chief of the Black eunuchs, to whom the citizens had recourse for justice against underlings. Wheler by means of transliterated tables shows that the Athenians not only pronounced Greek but wrote it as they do now.

Travellers then, as travellers now, were naturally in a great hurry to see the Parthenon, 'the finest single antiquity in the world', even if in general Rome was to be preferred. They had some difficulty in getting in, but finally prevailed upon the commander of the citadel to admit them for a consideration of three okes of coffee. Inside they found a straggling village, which housed the garrison of 100 resident irregulars, not Janissaries, whose duty it was to repel pirates. Wheler climbed the minaret, and noted the 'great planks of stone' of which the roof of the Parthenon was constructed.

The description of the Parthenon and its sculpture which both travellers give is basically Spon's. It is of the utmost value, because it is the only one we have of the sculptures before the temple was ruined. Spon and Wheler made their way to the Erechtheium as well, but were not allowed inside because the governor's *harem* lived in it, the spaces between the Caryatids having been filled in to make a continuously walled room. The remaining monuments were much as we see them now, except for the terminal of Hadrian's aqueduct, and a little Ionic temple built into a church by the Ilissus and the bridge over the Ilissus by the stadium, demolished to provide materials for the new wall built by the Turks in 1788, but all sketched by Stuart and Revett (see below). The Arch of Hadrian fortunately escaped: being on the lines of the wall, it was simply incorporated in it. The temple of Wingless Victory was dismantled in 1687 to provide space for a battery. Fortunately the stones were left on the site, and so it was possible to reconstruct the temple first in 1835, and then more accurately in 1936–40. It is thus the only temple to have been erected three times.

The year 1687 was fatal to the Akropolis. On 21 September the Venetians under Morosini, who commanded an army of German mercenaries led by Count Koenigsmark, landed at Piraeus and laid siege to Athens, on 26 September, at seven in the morning, Mutoni, who was in charge of the artillery, fired the fatal shot. It was no fluke: a deserter had informed Koenigsberg that the Turks were using the Parthenon as a magazine. The explosion was devastating. The roof, the massive walls of the cella, eight columns from the northern side and six from the southern side, together with much of the temple's sculpture crashed to the ground or was blown to bits. Thus in a second was destroyed a monument which had survived more than two thousand years.

A wholly new attitude to Athens and to Greece was inaugurated by the visit to the city of two Englishmen in the year 1751. They were James Stuart (1713–1788) and Nicholas Revett (1720–1804). In 1748 in Rome, where they had been studying painting, they met their fellow-countrymen Wood and Dawkins, on their way to explore Palmyra. On a journey to Naples, the explorers fired Revett with their enthusiasm. Why should not he and Stuart similarly explore Athens? The idea was novel, but it was eagerly taken up. It was backed by numerous friends and by the Society of Dilettanti.

The Dilettanti, founded in 1735, were a society of well-born young Englishmen, originally forty-six in number, who wanted to 'encourage at home a taste for those objects which had contributed so much to their enjoyment abroad'. The tone of the Society was frankly raffish. It included Sir Francis Dashwood, the Black Magician, the Earl of Sandwich, a notorious lecher who gave his name to a group of islands and to 'a familiar article of diet', Sir Hugh Smithson whose illegitimate son founded the Smithsonian Institution in Washington, William Berkeley who, having obtained the governorship of Virginia, ruled the colony so badly that he provoked an insurrection and the burning of Jamestown, the oldest English settlement in America. Later members were less gaudy and more classical. They included Sir William Hamilton, British Minister at Naples, who was largely responsible for the mission of Canova to Paris. His collection of vases – it included the famous Portland Vase – found its way directly or indirectly to the British Museum (opened in 1759); Charles Townley who gave his collection to the Museum in 1805; William Hamilton (no relation to Sir William) who arranged for many valuable Egyptian antiquities, including the Rosetta Stone to be ceded to England; Charles Cockerell

*Above*
Athens, looking at the
Akropolis from the temple of
Hephaistos.

*Left*
Spring flowers at Olympia.
The temple of Hera is in the
background.

The Resting Hermes, a fine replica now in Whewell's Court, Trinity College, Cambridge, where it looks quite at home in Salvin's mid-Victorian setting. The original, from the Villa of the Papyri in Herculaneum, is in the National Museum, Naples. The replica was placed in Cambridge half a century ago: an eloquent exposition of English philhellenism.

who discovered the temple at Bassae, and organized the acquisition of its sculptures for the British Museum – all of them were members of the Dilettanti.

Stuart and Revett stayed in Venice on their way to Athens. There they met Sir James Grey, an active Dilettante, and although Stuart was only the son of a seaman (Revett came of an old Suffolk family) both were elected into the Society.

The two men remained in Athens from 1751 until the end of 1753. Their method of working was new. Painters though they both were, they were not going to be content with 'picturesque views'. Their equipment included 'instruments made in London by the best Artists, one of which was a Rod of Brass, most accurately divided by Mr Bird'. Mr Bird's rod of brass was quite literally their yardstick. Sketches they did make, and most valuable they are; but what gives their published work its unique character is the precision of the measurements and the accuracy with which they are reproduced. Wood and Dawkins again gave them much help when they came to Athens on their way home from the Levant.

Proposals for publication were made in 1755, and seldom can a work have had such a remarkable list of subscribers. They were more than 600, and included peers, prelates, scholars, governors, consuls, architects, artists, builders and a 'plaisterer'. The elder Pitt, Horace Walpole, Sir Joshua Reynolds all subscribed. So did David Garrick and Peg Woffington. Among the foreign supporters were Benjamin Franklin and Luigi Vanvitelli. The first volume appeared in 1762. Although it did not show the Parthenon, which was included only in the second volume in 1788 – there would be four altogether – it was an instant success. Here at last was the authentic Grecian, the true original, no longer Roman copies. Stuart got the lion's share of the praise and was known as 'Athenian Stuart'. Revett naturally resented this, and withdrew from the enterprise; but both men were in great demand as architects. Revett built the church at Eyot St Lawrence, Stuart the chapel at Greenwich Hospital and 15 St James's Square, the first truly Grecian house in the town. For the rest of the century Grecian architecture was the mode, as the remains of Regency London still remind us. Europe followed the lead of the two Englishmen, and Charles Cameron carried the new ideas to Russia, where the buildings he created for Catherine the Great are among the glories of Leningrad. Not since Vitruvius had a single publication had so wide and lasting an effect upon architecture.

While Stuart and Revett were at work in Athens, Magna Graecia had been yielding up some of the finest examples of Greek sculpture, especially bronzes, ever to see the light: they had been buried ever since AD 79, when Herculaneum was overwhelmed by the volcano.

The spoilation of the buried city started in 1709, when (as so often) by chance Prince d'Elboeuf, as he was building himself a villa, descended a peasant's well-shaft and penetrated to the stage of a theatre. Had this been left untouched it would have been the finest surviving ancient theatre, because the stony lava had simply flowed over its upper edge and petrified everything *in situ*. But Elboeuf's investigations were ruinous, and the stage with its columns, polychrome marbles and statues was utterly destroyed.

Excavations began officially in 1738 (ten years before those at Pompeii), under the patronage of the Bourbon king Charles III of Naples and his enlightened minister Tanucci. The pits and tunnels then sunk – the day of opencast archaeology had not yet dawned – led to notable discoveries, of which the most remarkable, both for the daring of the tunnelling and the richness of its yield, was that of the so-called Villa of the Papyri, in a western suburb. Fortunately we possess a plan of the villa, and of the serpentine subterranean galleries which gave access to the exceptional wealth of papyri and bronze statues. These were abundant. The best known of them is the 'resting Hermes' of which a replica adorns Whewell's Court at Trinity College Cambridge.

While the mining was going on in 1763, a German called Johann Joachim Winckelmann visited the site. He was the son of a poor cobbler, but at the age of thirty-eight, with a notable publication, he had already attracted enthusiastic notice as a promoter of archaeology. He was entranced by what he saw at Herculaneum, and his report on it ensured his fame when it was published in 1764. In the same year appeared his masterpiece, the *Geschichte der Kunst des Altertums* (History of Ancient Art).

The book was widely popular. 'Winckelmannship' became a cult. No one now would take him as wholly authoritative. To cite but one example. Winckelmann was homosexual; when therefore he was able to contemplate the relief of Antinoüs which had been found in Hadrian's Villa in 1735, he went into raptures about 'Greek beauty'. Antinoüs was not a Greek: he came from Bithynia in Asia Minor. Ever since, Antinoüs has been a subject of controversy – aesthetic, moral, pyschological. So far as art is concerned – and it was the *art* of the ancients which Winckelmann made his province, the relevance of Antinoüs has been put with authority by Lord Clark in his *The Nude*: 'For almost the first time since the fourth century a type of beauty is taken from a real head and not from a copy-book . . . We feel once more though remotely enough, the warmth of an individual achievement . . . The physical character of Antinoüs is still perceptible when, after its long banishment, the Apollonian nude returns in the person of Donatello's David.'

Winckelmann was murdered in 1768 at Trieste at the age of fifty-one, by a greedy oaf to whom he had taken a foolish fancy, and to whom he had shewn some of the coins which the empress Maria Theresa had given him in Vienna. We are the losers; but by the time of his death, the pattern of archaeology had been stabilized. Henceforth it is to be an international persuit. It will assemble in rivalry and then in co-operation the perception of France, the self-confidence of England, the sensibility of Italy, the precision of Germany, and ultimately the enthusiasm of America, the heir of all the others. By the year 1800 archaeology has come of age.

Johann Joseph Winckelmann (1717–68). The father of modern archaeology.

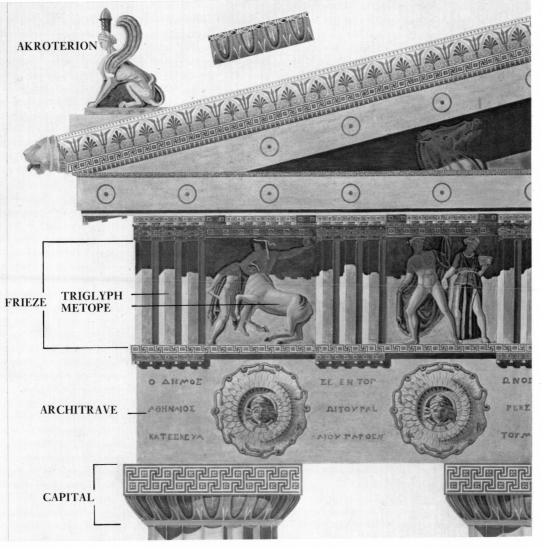

**AKROTERION**

**FRIEZE**

**TRIGLYPH
METOPE**

**ARCHITRAVE**

Ο ΔΗΜΟΣ

ΑΘΗΝΑΙΟΣ

ΚΑΤΕΣΚΕΥΑ

ΣΕ ΕΝ ΤΟΓ

ΛΙΤΟΥΡΓΑΙ

ΛΙΟΥ ΓΑΡΘΕΝ

Ω ΝΟΣ

ΠΕΡΕ

ΤΟΥΜ

**CAPITAL**

*Above*
Temples to Poseidon, god
of the sea, stood on many
promontories in ancient
Greece, and the most famous
is the one that stood on Cape
Sunium. It was a welcome
landmark for the returning
seamen of Athens: once
round the Cape they had their
first sight of home.

*Left*
The aspect of Greek
temples, after centuries of
neglect and exposure, led
many antiquarians to believe
that they always stood
unadorned, in gleaming
white marble. It is now
known that they were
elaborately decorated, as in
this hand-coloured
engraving from *Über
Anwendung der Farben in der
Baukunst* by Gottfried
Semper, Dresden, 1836.

*Opposite*
Head of a bronze statue
recovered from the sea off
Cape Artemision in 1928, and
believed to be of the god
Poseidon. It dates from the
mid-fifth century BC and is
now in the National
Museum, Athens.

The Venus de Milo. Louvre.

# CHAPTER II

# Hellas Unbound

'We are all Greeks. Our laws, our literature, our religion, our arts, have their root in Greece ...'

'The human form and the human mind attained to a perfection in Greece which has impressed its image on those faultless productions, whose very fragments are the despair of modern art, and has propagated impulses which cannot cease through a thousand channels of manifest or imperceptible operation, to ennoble and delight mankind until the extinction of the race.'

Thus wrote Shelley at Pisa in November 1821 in the preface to his last great work *Hellas*. The Greek war of Liberation had just started. The poem is a paean, confident in ultimate triumph. In this vision Shelley, who had never been in Greece, was a more committed prophet than his friend Byron, who had. When Shelley was drowned off Lerici, in July of the following year, Byron conducted the last rites there on the shore; but it was only in 1823 that he returned to Greece. He died at Missolonghi on 19 April 1824. Such was, and such remains, Byron's fame that although he did not in fact see any fighting, his mere presence in Greece had a magnetic effect on men's minds and actions. It is easy therefore to see Greek Independence as having been the crowning achievement of Byron the Liberator. The facts are far different. The struggle was long, the Greek cause opposed by nearly all the governments of Europe, including that of Britain. From March 1821, when Greek arms were first taken up against Turkey, until October 1827 when the battle of Navarino settled the question in the Greeks' favour, more than six terrible years were to pass, years marked by barbarism on both sides, by dissension within the Greek ranks and by apathy without. Volunteers came from many lands; France, Germany, the United States and England. England's contribution was by no means the largest numerically but it was one of the most effective, because apart from the magic of Byron's name England gave Greece a military leader in Richard Church and an admiral in Lord Cochrane who between them animated and resuscitated the Greek forces and led them to victory.

The powers of Europe, largely through mutual jealousy and suspicion, were now shamed into action.

When a new session of the English parliament was opened after Navarino, the Speech from the Throne referred to the battle as an 'untoward incident', such was England's craven fear of Russia and, its corollary, her desire to back Turkey at all costs. Nevertheless, the independence of Greece was finally recognized after protracted chaffering, mainly through the efforts of Canning, the English Prime Minister. He is still commemorated in Athens by the square which bears his name and the fine statue of him by Westmacott which stands there. In September 1829 the treaty of Adrianople established Greece (or rather the southern portion of it) as an independent monarchy.

The first, interim, ruler of the new Greece – which, even though it did not include the whole peninsula, was at least the very first unitary Greek state in all history – was Count Capo d'Istria whose portrait by Lawrence adorns the Waterloo Chamber at Windsor Castle. That is because he was the Foreign Minister of the Tsar before he became the first ruler of Greece, an international figure before he became a Greek patriot. Capo d'Istria was an excellent governor. They called him simply *kybernites* (helmsman) as befitted the head of a seafaring race; but he was assassinated in October 1831. Anarchy ensued, checked only by the arrival of the lad whom the powers, England, France, and Russia, had chosen to be the new king, seventeen-year-old Otho, son of the most frenzied Philhellene in Europe, king Ludwig I of Bavaria, who had secured the Aegina marbles for Munich.

Shelley could not possibly have foreseen this outcome of the Greek revolt. His confidence, therefore, is all the more remarkable. It shews us just how wide, how deep, the love of Hellas had grown. Shelley's reference to the 'very fragments' which were the 'despair of modern art' is significant. By 1821, the three greatest expatriate treasures of Greek sculpture had reached their new homes. The Elgin marbles had been bought by the nation in 1816. (For £35,000: they had cost Lord Elgin £74,000 from first to last.) The Bassae frieze had been acquired for £15,000 by the Prince Regent, and Ludwig had his Aegina sculptures for £6,000. These last

George Gordon, 6th Baron Byron, 1788–1824. This statue, the only one of Byron done from life, is the work of the Danish sculptor Albert Thorwaldsen (1770–1844). It was made in Rome in 1817 when Byron was twentynine. Offered to (but rejected by) Westminster Abbey, it now adorns the library of Byron's old college, Trinity, Cambridge.

*Overleaf*
The great rock, Akrocorinth, the original citadel of the city of Corinth. In the foreground are the ruins of the temple of Apollo, one of the earliest Doric temples, dating from the middle of the fifth century BC. The columns, nearly twenty-four feet high, are each carved from a single piece of stone.

The temple of Apollo at Bassae. The architect was Iktinos, the builder of the Parthenon. Late fifth century BC.

Thorwaldsen, the fashionable Danish sculptor who produced the only statue of Byron to be done from life, now in the library of Trinity College, Cambridge, drastically 'restored'.

One incident may demonstrate how providential the saving of these masterpieces, whether viewed as 'protective custody' or not, turned out to be. It is, as it were, the colophon on the eighteenth century's idea of archaeology as sanctified loot. It is given in a letter from Charles Cockerell, the discoverer of the Bassae and Aegina marbles. He had been on good terms with the Turkish garrison commander on the Akropolis, who decided to give his English friend a parting present.

'As he knew I was very fond of old sculptured stones he asked me if I would like to bring a cart to the base of the Acropolis at a certain hour of the night. I accordingly arranged this. As I drew near the Acropolis there was a shout from above to look out, and without further warning the block which formed one of the few remaining pieces of the southern frieze of the Parthenon was bowled down the cliff. My men successfully caught it and put it in the cart and it was taken to Piraeus and loaded that same night onto my ship.'

Charles Robert Cockerell deserves a word or two to himself. He was born in 1788, the second son of Samuel Pepys Cockerell, a rich man who was an architect in the service of the East India Company. He left Westminster school at sixteen, and joined his father's office. After an architectural tour of England he entered the office of Robert Smirke, the architect of the British Museum, and in 1809 was sent off on a tour of Greece and Turkey. William Hamilton, Lord Elgin's secretary, was a friend of the family

and arranged the journey: Cockerell was to go as a King's Messenger to the Royal Navy at Cadiz, Malta and Constantinople. In the Turkish capital Cockerell met Lord Byron and his friend Hobhouse. He caroused with Lord Byron, visited the sights without much enthusiasm and called on the ambassador, Lord Canning, whom he found 'too grand'. In December 1810 Cockerell and a young architect from Liverpool called Foster arrived in Athens, and immediately became members of the gay galaxy of which Byron was the sun.

April 1811 saw Cockerell and his band of friends in Aegina. They pitched their tents at the top of the hill, just by the temple. The shrine was well preserved, and a crop of barley growing on its floor gave it a pleasantly rustic look. For twenty days the young explorers stayed there, making drawings of the temple. Luck was theirs from the first. On the second day after their arrival, one of their labourers came across a 'piece of marble'. Marble in a limestone building: it must be of importance. It turned out to be the undamaged head of a helmeted warrior. Cockerell and his companions were entranced. Excavations were started, and yielded no less than sixteen torsos, thirteen heads and a collection of legs, arms and other fragments, all lying about a metre below the surface.

The populace and the Turkish authorities were naturally excited by this strange find. Nevertheless, Cockerell succeeded in hiring a caique, and smuggled the marbles away to Athens by night, he himself remaining on the island apparently still engaged in excavation until he heard that the loot was safe in Athens. Cockerell then paid off the workmen and gave the Pasha of the Islands a sum of forty guineas for 'digging rights'.

On reaching Athens, Cockerell decided that only under British protection would his marbles be safe, so once again they were smuggled away by night, from a small fishing village on the Gulf of Corinth – not from the Piraeus, where all cargoes were liable to surveillance. Their destination was the island of Zante, at that time under British occupation. A British warship arrived the next year to take the marbles to England, where the Prince Regent was willing to pay £6,000 for them. The captain of the ship was furious when he heard that the marbles were at Zante; it was no place, he said, to leave valuable marbles during wartime. They must be sent to Malta.

Meanwhile their auction had been advertised, to take place *in Zante* on 1 November 1812. When the time for the auction came round, the British Museum representative, knowing that the marbles were in Malta, went to that island, thinking that where the marbles were there would the sale be also. He was wrong, probably tricked. When the auction did, as advertised, take place in Zante no British bidder was on hand, and so the marbles went to the agent of prince, afterwards king, Ludwig I of Bavaria. They were taken to Munich, where despite unavailing attempts by Cockerell to invalidate the sale they still are.

*Above*
Count John Antonio Capo d'Istria, 1776–1831, a member of an ancient Corfiote family ennobled by the Venetians. He was the first elected ruler of united Greece, 1827, and assassinated in 1831.

*Left*
An example of the frieze from the temple of Apollo at Bassae, now in the British Museum. The subject is the combat between Greeks and Amazons.

This striking early nineteenth-century sketch in the Bibliothèque Nationale shows the Akropolis and the 'Theseum' in a splendid isolation they no longer possess. The 'Frankish Tower' was removed in 1875, at Schliemann's personal expense.

27

*Right*
One of the enormous earthenware storage vessels (*pithoi*) found at the Minoan site at Mallia, Crete.

*Far right*
The palace of Knossos. The balcony with the fresco is on the north side. Remnants of the columns of the hypostyle room can be seen in the foreground.

Phaistos, the great courtyard of the Minoan palace. The view looks north to Mount Ida.

Meanwhile Cockerell, rather than loiter in Zante awaiting the auction, had set out on a journey into the Peloponnese. Here he was to fare better. Having left Zante for Pyrgos on the Peloponnesian coast the party walked by way of Olympia to Bassae. This remote temple, designed by Iktinos, one of the architects of the Parthenon, had been visited by a French traveller in 1765 and was reputed to be a splendid example of Doric architecture. Disregarding the warnings of the local peasants, who warned them against bandits, Cockerell and his friends visited Bassae, which they found full of interest. The temple is indeed unique, with its Ionic half-columns engaged into the inner wall of the cella, and its Doric peristyle, dominating a still wild landscape at an altitude of 4,000 feet above sea level. The temple also employed pillars (or at least one) with a Corinthian capital, the earliest known used functionally, and this was the first temple to use all three orders. The fabric is limestone, the frieze marble.

Cockerell spent ten days making drawings and taking measurements, which he hoped to publish in a book on reaching England, thus rivalling the fame of Stuart and Revett. The excavations, however, were completely fruitless, and the party were preparing to quit when one morning Cockerell noticed a fox emerging from a mass of fallen blocks in the interior of the temple. 'I went in carefully,' wrote Cockerell to his father, 'lest there be another fox, and on scraping away the accumulations where the fox had its lair, I saw by the light which came down a crack among the stones, a bas-relief. We made a rough sketch of the bas-relief and covered it up again.'

They decided to come back again next spring, and so returned to Athens to face the disappointment over the Aegina marbles related above. Cockerell then set out on a tour of Asia Minor, but his friends went back to Bassae in the spring of 1812. Gropius, the Austrian consul, whose mother was Greek, had secured the necessary permits, both local and from the Porte, to excavate. The excavations were a great success; and although Cockerell was not present it was agreed that he should have an equal share in the finds, being the discoverer of the original bas-relief. All the treasures were to be put up for auction at Zante; but a difficulty was that the Englishmen and their German colleagues had promised the local Turkish governor one half of their spoils. While they were debating what to do, they learned that the governor was to be transferred. They at once offered him £400 as a quit-rent,

29

which he eagerly accepted. The marbles were then transported over the mountains down to the coast. They were all safely on board a ship bound for Zante, with the exception of the Corinthian capital, when the new governor, feeling himself swindled out of what he felt should be his cut, appeared with a troop of soldiers to stop the proceedings. The ship at once set sail, leaving the Turks on the shore so enraged that they hacked the capital to bits there on the strand where it stood half in and half out of water.

The auction was fixed for May 1814, and all the leading continental newspapers were informed. This time there was no mistake. The sculptures were knocked down to an agent of the Prince Regent for £6,000, and safely reached the British Museum, where they are now on view.

Cockerell arrived back in England in 1817, having taken seven years over a trip which his father had planned to cover only one. He now had to return to his father's office. All his plans for publication were

Inside the temple of Aphaea, Aegina.

frustrated, his own book delayed, his plans and sketches pirated. His chief memorials in England are the Ashmolean Museum at Oxford, which he designed, and the gilded ball and cross atop Wren's St Paul's in London, which he renovated. But he is honoured by being placed between Barry and Pugin on the Albert Memorial in Kensington.

Meanwhile the French felt that they had not only been left behind but defrauded in the artistic treasure-hunt. The famous horses had gone back to Venice. The Rosetta stone was in England, the Laocoön and the Belvedere Apollo were in Rome again. All that France had secured was a fragment or two of the Parthenon frieze and two metopes, obtained by Choiseul-Gouffier, an enterprising French ambassador.

Through him a taste for things Greek was stimulated in the United States. Thomas Jefferson saw in Paris some plaster models which Choiseul-Gouffier had had made, including one of the Maison Carée in Nîmes. Jefferson used this as the basic model for the statehouse in Richmond, Virginia, substituting Ionic for Corinthian capitals, because he felt that the more intricate Corinthian design would be beyond the skills at that time available in his home state.

Then, in 1820, the little island of Melos provided France with a treasure, a real prize: the famous 'Venus de Milo'. Nothing could be more 'French' than its discovery. There it was, an unidentified nude female, in two pieces, in a remote island, surrounded by mystery and intrigue. After a century and a half, we still do not know who actually found the statue, whether he found it with arms attached, or detached, or with no arms in the vicinity. Its ownership was disputed, a battle for its possession took place on the harbour-front; it was more than a year en route before it reached the Louvre. That the acquisition did much to salve French pride is as certain as that the statue itself caressed French taste. To-day, in its perfectly lighted stance in the Louvre, it gives, be it an early work or a late one, a thrill of delight to all who come upon it; and a conviction that the Louvre is the one place where it is most suitably sheltered. 'Cherchez la femme'? You need go no farther.

The other great classical female sculpture in the Louvre presents a striking contrast to the famous Aphrodite, or Venus (if that is who she really is). Whereas the earlier find was made much of, to put it mildly, the Winged Victory of Samothrace lay for decades unregarded. Samothrace is a beautiful island. Like its neighbour Thasos, it is northern rather than Mediterranean, clothed with green woods. The island had been renowned ever since the Trojan War, because as Homer tells us it was from the summit of Samothrace, 5,000 feet above the sea, that Poseidon had watched the conflict. Postulants and pilgrims flocked to it from all over the Hellenic world bearing rich gifts to the shrine of the Cabiri, mysterious and potent spirits of the deep. Very daring and determined they must have been, because Pliny tells us that Samothrace was the 'most harbourless' island of them all, as it still is: visitors are lucky if they are able to land. Paul of Tarsus called there on his way from Asia to Europe, and

there, above the theatre, he must have seen the now famous Victory.

In 1858 a German student called Conze landed at Samothrace, noticed some ruins in a valley, but thought them of no consequence. In 1862 a young French consul from Adrianople, Champoiseau by name, went there, and was much impressed by what he saw. The French government, always readier than others to promote the fine arts, gave him a grant to start his excavations. It was then that the statue was discovered. According to his own report, Champoiseau came on a fragment of marble in the ground, and clearing the soil from it, found it to be (as a good Frenchman would) 'the most beautifully shaped woman's breast'. Two feet below, a goddess came to light 'whose pose and outstretched wings identified her as Victory'. But as the statue was found in some two hundred pieces, it is hard to see how its finder recognized the 'pose' or the identity of the sculpture.

A figure from the Aegina marbles, as 'restored' by Thorwaldsen. National Museum, Munich.

Mycenae. The grave circle as
it appears today, looking
south.

With the statue were also found twenty-six large
marble blocks of unusual shape, which Champoiseau
ignored. The French ambassador at the Porte
(Samothrace was still part of the Ottoman
dominions) sent a naval vessel to collect the statue,
which duly arrived in France. It excited little interest
in the Louvre. It took three years to reassemble, and
was then relegated as a 'mediocre decorative figure
of late period' to one of the darkest corners of the

Museum. One or two experts did recognize its value,
and a second expedition was sent to Samothrace in
1866. It was a complete failure. Conze then returned
to work on the island; but he too saw no importance
in the twenty-six blocks. Only when sketches and
notes taken on this last expedition were being edited
for publication in Vienna did an Austrian savant
realize what he was looking at. It was, he saw, a
pedestal in the shape of a ship's prow, and exactly

corresponded with a coin struck in 306 BC by Demetrios Polioketes to celebrate a victory off Salamis of Cyprus, which made him lord of that island. A fierce battle then raged as to who had identified the blocks, the Frenchman or the Austrian? France won, and in 1879 the blocks reached Paris. Even then, the statue, back on its pedestal, remained poked away hugger-mugger for another fifteen years. In all, it lay in the Louvre unregarded for thirty-four years. Only in 1896 was it promoted to its splendid eminence on the grand staircase. If ever statue embodied *La Gloire* it is the Winged Victory; and so, as with the goddess of Melos it is appropriate that it should adorn the capital of a nation to whom *La Gloire* means so much.

Already, by 1830, these tales of statue-rustling, of which we have just contemplated the last, had become as obsolete as their cattle counterparts in the wild American West. Archaeology was now respectable; and the reason for its reformation is to be found in the Greeks themselves. 'Another Athens shall arise', Shelley had foretold all those years ago,

> Another Athens shall arise
>   And to remoter time
> Bequeath, like sunset to the skies,
>   The splendour of its prime;
> And leave, if nought so bright may live,
>   All earth can take or heaven give.

Otho's reign ended sadly. The Crimean war in which two of his 'protectors', England and France, had sided with the traditional foe, Turkey, against the third 'protector', Russia, had undermined the loyalty of his subjects. In 1862 he was deposed, and returned to Bavaria, where he died four years later. He was only fifty-two and had been a king for thirty-one years. His days of sovereignty had bestowed many benefits on resurgent Hellas.

In 1832 Athens was in ruins. Its inhabitants were refugees once more, and the Akropolis was still occupied by a Turkish garrison, which was only dislodged the next year. Gradually the citizens returned, and life began afresh. The young king's architects, German and Greek, at once set about laying down the town-plan which has given modern Athens its spacious streets and convenient squares. The master-planner was Leo von Klenze, the design, as we now see it, the work of Kleanthes and Schaubert. These artists were proudly conscious of their privileged task, which was to recreate Athens. Both Otho and his queen, Amalia of Oldenburg, were deeply imbued with a love of their adopted country, and the neo-classical buildings erected under their auspices have real charm, akin to that of the Gothic of Pugin and Barry in England.

Naturally the ancient monuments were not neglected: even more than the new creations they were to be the heart of the new Athens. Almost at once an archaeological service was organized, and by one of the very first laws to be passed in 1832, the export of artistic remains of aesthetic or archaeological value was prohibited. The Akropolis was gradually cleared. It had suffered considerably during the fighting, the Erechtheium in particular hav-

The Victory of Samothrace. Louvre.

A section of the Elgin
Marbles, fragments of the
sculptures by Pheidias which
adorned the frieze and
pediment of the Parthenon.
British Museum.

ing been almost wrecked by artillery fire; and the bodies of those who had perished in the debris were not recovered until 1832. The Parthenon too was hit. What would have been the fate of the famous sculptures if they had been still exposed to shell-fire?

At one time it had been proposed that the Akropolis should house the royal palace; but the royal couple lived in a house on the site of what is now the National Historical Museum. What is called the 'Old Palace' above Syntagma Square was built for them in 1836. Otho's father Ludwig shared in the expense of its construction, not yet having lost his fortune and his throne through his infatuation with Lola Montez. Queen Amalia's personal contribution to the restored capital was a pretty little Belvedere in the north-west corner of the Akropolis, which when it was built must have commanded a splendid view of Attica and its mountains. Amalia also, less commendably, had the stone panels removed from the upper story of Hadrian's Arch, to make it look more 'picturesque'.

Under the Turkish régime, the whole area of the Akropolis had been usurped by a squalid village, in which the Turkish military commandant had his headquarters. All these accretions were now cleared away. The minaret was pulled down, the mosque in the Parthenon dismantled. The stones of the temple of Wingless Victory, which had been demolished to form a bulwark at the time of Morosini's invasion, now came to light, and the shrine was erected for the second time. The Venetian batteries, the Turkish bastions, all were removed. Finally in 1875 the 'Frankish' or Florentine tower at the Propylaea was abolished at the expense of Schliemann himself. These labours were to continue for years, and are still in hand. The Greeks have a word for the process, namely *anastylosis*, meaning the putting up of pillars; though it is doubtful whether the surviving fabric of the major monuments could bear the strain of any further restoration. The Temple of Wingless Victory however was carefully taken down and erected for yet a third time in the thirties of this century much to its advantage. The result is that despite the ravages of war, vandalism and theft we now possess once more the four great monuments of the Golden Age, that is the Temple of Winged Victory, the Propylaea, the Parthenon and the Erechtheium.

To this we can now add the recovery of the Dipylon Gate and the Kerameikos, largely by German enterprise, and the clearance and restoration of the Agora and Stoa of Attalus, the gift of American munificence and skill.

Archaeology is now international. Many nations have established schools in Athens. Those of the United States and England share the same garden and each other's libraries. The American School also administers the great collections of the patriot-diplomatist Gennadios. The Greek government welcomes this international comradeship and participation. Each recognized school may be granted up to three licences to excavate each year. The treasures of the past and the patrimony of the future are being continually enriched and augmented.

# Olympia

The resurgent Greeks had shewn that, if in their political activities they sometimes lacked the touch of a Perikles, their aesthetic perception (for that is what the word aesthetic means) was as sensitive as ever that of their ancestors had been. Athens was now secure, and its ancient glories were on the way to rejuvenation. The city would once again be a lighthouse for Europe; but rather to the surprise of Europeans the Greeks felt that its first rays should illumine their own land. The prohibition of the export of antiquities has already been mentioned; but even before the establishment of the kingdom, the provisional government had stopped a French expedition from further excavation of one of the most important of Greek sites, Olympia. Throughout the world, no ancient sanctuary was more widely known than this sacred precinct in the north-western Peloponnese. It was universally famous because it was at Olympia that the great Panhellenic Games had been celebrated. Their original pacific purpose has been blurred by their unfortunate 'revival' in 1896, so that the modern Olympic Games, the focus of every sort of national arrogance, rancour and chicanery, have wholly obscured the peaceful, unifying aim of the original institution.

Like so much in Greek life, the origin of the Games, here as elsewhere, is wreathed in myth. Who had started them – Herakles, was it? Or Pelops? No one was sure. But by the beginning of the sixth century BC there were four established Games festivals; the Pythian, celebrated at Delphi, those of Nemea, near Argos, the Isthmian, held on the Isthmus of Corinth, and the Olympic. Of these the Olympic held undisputed primacy, because their first organized celebration could be traced back the year 776 BC, and the four-yearly intervals between the meetings gave rise to the chronological reckoning by Olympiads, the only generally accepted unit of time throughout the Greek world, because each state reckoned its own epoch by office-holders; the eponymous archon at Athens for instance, or by the years of a sovereign's reign, as English acts of parliament still do. The Christian church historian of the fourth century AD, Eusebius, citing Julius Africanus of Jerusalem, has preserved a list of all the

Olympic winners from 776 BC to AD 221. In the third century BC Eratosthenes of Cyrene claimed that the historic age of Hellas, as distinct from the mythical, began with the beginning of the Olympic era in 776 BC. The use of Olympiads as chronological intervals may be as early as the fifth century.

The year of foundation, or reorganization, and periodicity of the other games is as follows: Pythian, in the third year of each Olympiad after 582; Isthmian, every second year after 581; Nemean, in the second and fourth year of each Olympiad after 573.

The importance of the Olympic Games, other than to the winners, was that they were the main, almost the only, truly international event of the Hellenic world. The little Greek states were extremely litigious. The best known and most disastrous conflict was that between Athens and Sparta in the latter half of the fifth century; but minor squabbles were endemic. It was only at the Games, for which a special truce was observed, proclaimed by heralds despatched to all quarters, that any Greek could be sure of immunity from molestation by those with whom he was at feud, and on his way there and back he would be sacrosanct. No armed men might pass through Olympia. In 420 the Lacedaemonians were excluded from the festival for truce-breaking, Thucydides tells us. The Games thus came to attract competitors from all over the Greek world, including very notably the opulent Greek west, of Sicily and southern Italy. Of the eleven 'treasuries' (or chapel-consulates) of which traces survive at Olympia, six are the gifts of western Greek states.

Competitors were required to have undergone at least a year's training, of which the final month must be passed at Olympia itself, under the scrutiny of official trainers. Amateur status was ostentatiously, if deceptively, maintained. The winners were crowned with wild olive only. (At the Pythian, with bay, and with wild parsley at the Nemean and Isthmian). But a victor's home town rewarded him handsomely. Athenian victors were fed at the state's expense in the Town Hall. It is said that one town even pulled down a section of its wall, so that the

champion athlete might enter by a gate never before trodden by man. In the fifth century it was not yet customary to erect statues to great statesmen or generals but the *Olympionikai*, as they were called, had the right to put up a statue of bronze or marble of themselves in the sacred precinct, and to demand an ode to be composed for public recitation.

The most famous of these songs were and have remained those of Pindar. He was born in 518 near Thebes, and always considered himself a Theban, although his precocious poetical talent early led him into many parts of the Hellenic world, including all four festival centres. He was in great demand as a writer of triumphal odes, and very well he did by them. Athens paid him 10,000 drachmas for a eulogy of the city, and made him an honorary magistrate. He travelled as far as Sicily; and it is a striking testimony to the wealth of the west that of the forty-four triumphal odes of his that have come down to us, no less than fifteen were dedicated to Sicilians, with Aegina, a favourite residence of Pindar, runner-up with only fourteen.

The Games took place in July, when the days were long, the harvest had been garnered, and sailing conditions were at their best. It was timed to coincide with the full moon, which provided illumination after sunset. The whole festival occupied a month, of which the fourth week was the grand climax.

*Above*
Olympia. The Palaestra, or wrestling school, in which competitors finished their training under official supervision. Third century BC.
*Right*
The temple of Hera, looking west. The oldest (the beginning of the seventh century BC) and best preserved of the temples of Olympia. The original structure was of wood, and this was gradually replaced by stone.

Competitors had to be freeborn Greeks, of unblemished character; but many others assembled for the gathering. Besides the athletes, the great concourse included poets, philosophers and men of letters. Herodotus went to Olympia to recite portions of his history. Living conditions must have been squalid. The sacred enclosure or *Altis* – the word means a grove – lies at the junction of the river Alphaeus, a broad perennial stream which comes down from the mountains of Arcadia, and a tributary called the Cladeus. Bathing and swimming would be possible, as they still are, and fresh water would have been abundant. Even so the assembly of thousands of folk from all over Hellas and beyond, cramped in makeshift encampments (save for official guests who were lodged in a hostel, and the competitors who had their own quarters) must have generated considerable filth and stench. Sanitation only came with the Romans. Flies were everywhere, and Pausanias tells us of special sacrifices offered to Zeus, Lord of Flies, to keep them at bay. Small wonder that the actual contests lasted five days only, and that an interval of four years was allowed for the contaminated ground to become sweet again, and the plane trees which then shaded the *Altis* to recover their foliage, devastated as they were to furnish the campers' booths.

The first day of the Games proper was allotted to registration and to religious exercises, because the Games were primarily a religious occasion. The contests started on the second day, with a horse-race on the now eroded hippodrome down by the river-bank, followed by the pentathlon of five events, running, long-jump, discus-throwing, javelin-hurling and wrestling. The third day was devoted to sacrifice and junior events for boys. On the fourth day came more foot-races, wrestling, boxing, all-in wrestling and a race in armour. The fifth and last day was given over to feasting and jollification. No women were present, except one priestess of Demeter, a venerable matron who sat enthroned above the stadium. The competitors, at least after the fifth century, ran naked; though some modern champions have doubted whether this involved complete nudity, on the ground that the male anatomy would be subjected to inconvenience and discomfort if it were wholly bereft of support.

Cheating was common. After all, it was successful cheating by Pelops which had given him his bride, as related in the pedimental sculpture described below. A special area was devoted to the statues for which detected delinquents had to pay. They were called *Zanes*, a local dialect name of Zeus. The bases of sixteen such statues have been found in front of the terraces where the treasuries stood.

The Games early lost their pristine simplicity and amateur status. Euripides inveighed against the insolent race of athletes. But the meeting retained its international prestige. Philip of Macedon and his son Alexander the Great embellished the sanctuary, and so did their successors. Even Mummius, the Roman general who destroyed Corinth in 146 BC, gave twenty-one gold-plated shields to be placed on the temple of Zeus. Sulla, on the other hand, pillaged the shrine and carried off many of its treasures to

Rome. Herod the Great of Judaea, who had himself been a notable athlete in his youth, hearing that the Games had fallen on evil days, stepped in and became their patron and president. Nero, in AD 67, had a narrow escape in the hippodrome. He fell from his chariot, and was nearly crushed to death. This infers that he was in collision with another competitor, a legitimate hazard of the course, and that he became entangled in the reins, which were normally knotted behind the driver's back, so as to give him better 'braking-power' over fresh steeds. Nero was awarded the first prize, despite this mishap, and recompensed the organizers with the huge sum of 400,000 sesterces. He also built himself a villa with a triumphal arch in the south-east corner of the sanctuary.

Olympia knew an autumnal flowering under Hadrian (117–138) who was a genuine philhellene. Herodes Atticus, the rich friend of Marcus Aurelius, contributed baths and an aqueduct in 174.

Then the decline set in. People still went to Olympia, but it was to a tourist resort, no longer to a shrine. Fortunately for us a Greek called Pausanias wrote a guide-book to Greece in the latter half of the second century AD. He has been rightly described as the Baedeker of the period. (See the excellent, annotated, translation by Peter Levi, S.J. in the Penguin Classics, 1971. This book is indispensable to any student of ancient Hellas). It is to Pausanias that we owe the accurate description of the precinct which so helped the excavators.

At the end of the third century invaders from the north threatened the sanctuary, and the priests destroyed many buildings in order to help throw up a makeshift wall round the main buildings in which they secreted many of their most precious posses-

The stadium where the ancient Olympic games were held was completely restored to the form it took in 45 BC by the German Institute, working from 1958 to 1962. The raised banks could accommodate 40,000 spectators. The starting and finishing lines are still there, 600 Olympic feet (192 metres) apart. The water channel and the remains of the judges' box are clearly visible.

*Above*
Zeus carries off Ganymede.
An archaic terracotta in the
Olympia Museum.

*Right*
Further details of the west
pediment of the temple of
Zeus. Apollo can be seen
quelling the centaurs who are
assaulting the Lapiths.

sions. The Games were formally abolished by an edict of Theodosius I in AD 393. Olympia, after a life of more than a millenium, was dead. Earthquakes and inundations of the two rivers, helped by the intrusion of a Byzantine village in the sixth century, lay waste the sacred grove. The flooding was a blessing, because it wrought an earthen pall of between seven to ten metres deep over the ruins. The hill called Kronion, above the stadium, eroded to half its original height, assisted the silting process.

For more than a thousand years, Olympia remained unidentified and unregarded. But not forgotten. Scholars read Pausanias. In 1723 the great French antiquarian Montfaucon tried unsuccessfully to persuade Cardinal Quirini, the Latin archbishop of Corfu, to explore it. Winckelmann himself projected an Olympian expedition in mid-century, but was murdered before he could visit Greece. The site was in fact found by an Englishman, Richard Chandler, in 1766. Chandler was a good Greek scholar of Magdalen College and had been chosen by the Dilettanti Society to accompany Nicholas Revett and another on an expedition to Ionia. Their discoveries were published as *Ionian*

*Antiquities* in 1769 – volume I, that is; the second and third volumes followed at intervals of twenty years, and the fourth only appeared in 1877. Before returning to England, Chandler had visited Athens, and Olympia too. From the Erechtheium he rescued an inscription, but found at Olympia nothing to detain or reward him. In 1811 Cockerell, as already related, was similarly not impressed, and hurried on to Bassae.

Then in 1814 a French savant, Antoine Chrystostome Quatremère de Quincy (1755–1849) published his book *Le Jupiter Olympien*. De Quincy's reputation in the learned world was almost equal to that of Winckelmann; and so interest, specially that of his countrymen, was at last aroused to the importance of the shrine of which the great statue had been the chief ornament.

The opportunity came in 1829, when an official French commission, attached, as was the excellent French custom, to the military force which had occupied the Peloponnese during the war against Turkey, started to excavate the temple of Zeus and succeeded in carrying off several metopes which are now in the Louvre. That was where the provisional

Gold among all worldly goods, the sun among the celestial bodies – thus does the poet exalt the primacy of Olympia. Here only in Greece can you walk in the shade of the pine-trees, listen to the nightingales and gaze upon the tawny relics of nobility set amid flowers of many hues. The other facet of Olympia's charm is its vitality. The ruins themselves seem not dead but sleeping. They are far less formal than the Akropolis, which is a deliberate and very successful essay in grandeur. Unlike the Athenian buildings which were the product of but half a century, the sanctuary here at Olympia was many hundreds of years a-growing; nor was any attempt ever made to enforce uniformity.

The older of the two temples, that of Hera, preaches against it. Its columns are of different diameters, as stone came to replace the original wood; the capitals vary in style, the flutings in number. In Pausanias' day, an ancient wood pillar was protected under cover; it was said to have come from the house of Oinomaus, not from Hera's temple, but it could be co-eval with it. The temple in its present form goes back to the seventh century BC. How venerable it is, how alive. And it was in this temple that in 1877 was found the famous Hermes of Praxiteles. Pausanias says that the statue was in the temple; but as to the authenticity of the figure found by the Germans and now in the Museum, it is best to quote Fr Levi's note:

'The famously smooth and skilful "Hermes of Praxiteles" in the Olympia Museum. Its pedestal is Hellenistic or Roman, the legs except for the right foot are modern; the conception is that of Praxiteles working about 325 BC, and the finish is glittering, but this is not the original statue; it is a fine Hellenistic copy. This sad but important truth is argued irrefutably by Sheila Adam in *The Technique of Greek Sculpture* (1966), pp. 124–8. Vol. 2, p. 248, n. 164.'

government stepped in and stopped the dig.

Only in 1875 was a treaty, the first of its kind, and the model for countless other agreements since that date, concluded between Greece and Germany, which allowed the latter to undertake systematic exploration of the site, on condition that all the finds remained in Greece.

One of the first actions of the Germans was to plant the pine trees which now make the *Altis* a grove once more, and one of the most restful and beautiful sites in all Greece.

The treasure of Olympia for us to-day is twofold. First, there is the shrine, with its two temples. The older one is that of Hera, the grander that of Zeus. Pindar, at the beginning of his first Olympian ode thus apostrophizes the sanctuary:

'If the prime element of well-being is water [as Thales of Miletus had taught] it is gold glistening like a flame kindled in the night which blots out all the treasures to overweaning wealth. Wouldst thou sing of the Games, my soul? Do not seek in the sky, forlorn when dayspring shines, a star more bright than the sun; nor hope to celebrate a contest more glorious than that of Olympia.'

Metope from the cella frieze of the temple of Zeus, which represents the Twelve Labours of Herakles. Here he is supporting the sky while Atlas holds out to him the golden apples of the Hesperides. A Hesperidaean nymph helps Herakles in his task.

A long acquaintance with the statue may well lead
to acceptance of this judgement.

The temple of Zeus was the dominating shrine,
the most important shrine in Greece (of Greece's
most important god, Zeus, who dwelt on Olympus
and gave the sanctuary its name). It was the work of a
local architect called Libon, and was dedicated in
457 BC. It is now a complete ruin. There it lies in
abject majesty, with not one stone standing upon
another. Its columns of the Doric order are the same
size as those of the Parthenon. The stone looks rough,
and is rough, but in its heyday it was covered with a
layer of stucco, of which traces remain, and which
was bright with colour. The sculptures from the
shrine have been recovered almost in their entirety,
and except for the metopes in the Louvre are now
displayed in the Olympia Museum. One pediment,
the west, depicts the fierce struggle between the
centaurs, half horse and half man, and the Lapiths,
a wild people of Thessaly. At the wedding of
Peirithoüs, king of the Lapiths, the centaurs got
drunk and assaulted the young maidens and lads,
until Apollo, one of the serenest representations of
deity ever fashioned, intervened to quell their beast-
liness. The subject was a favourite with the Greeks,
illustrating as it does the triumph of reason and
humanity over animal passion and violence.

The eastern pediment shewed the myth which
explained the origin of the Games. It is the prepara-
tion for the chariot-race in which Pelops, suitor for
the hand of Hippodameia ('Tamer of horses'), cheats
and beats her odious father (who had challenged
previous suitors to a horse-race, and then hanging
back had shot them from behind) by bribing the
coachman to remove the lynchpin from the king's
chariot.

Taken together, these two groups, together with
the metopes, form the most varied, most vivid,
group in all Greek surviving classical sculpture.

In the cella of this temple the masterpiece of
Pheidias, his Olympian Zeus, presided. It was
fashioned of gold and ivory, and was forty feet high.
The statue is lost. It was taken by Constantine
to his New Rome, Constantinople, and there
perished by fire in AD 475. The bedding of the
pedestal survives, and in front of it a large sunken
rectangle in the cella floor which once contained a
pool of oil, of which the function was to reflect the
statue and to counteract humidity and keep the
ivory from cracking. The German excavators found
the studio of Pheidias, which they deduced must be
his because its dimensions were exactly the same as
those of the cella. Their conjecture was confirmed
by the discovery there of a little cup with Pheidias'
name neatly inscribed on it. They also found the very
moulds used for making the gold plating. The thin
sheets could be hammered over them to fit the folds
of the statue's drapery. Some of them were marked
with serial letters on the back to show where they
were to fit into the pattern. Another workroom
nearby yielded the core of an elephant tusk, from
which ivory had been cut to repair the statue.

This temple also housed other remarkable
statuary, a Victory alighting, and a terracotta Zeus
with Ganymede, among them.

Only in the second half of the nineteenth century
was the great stadium itself identified, and only in the
second half of the present one has it been wholly
restored to us. It is entered through a tunnel, or
*krypte*, of the first century BC, one of the earliest
known Hellenic vaults. The stadium as we see it
to-day dates from the fourth century BC, having
succeeded two earlier structures. The course was
192 metres long. The ends were squared, not curved
as in Roman and modern stadia. The sides were
slightly concave, so that all front-line spectators
could get an unimpeded view.

The embankments concealed a marvellous cache
of discarded archaic armour, unique in its diversity
and abundance: helmets, including one bearing the
name of the great Miltiades, who beat the Persians
at Marathon in 490 BC, breastplates, greaves, shields,
embossed arm-straps for shields, unique armguards.
The devices on the shield-straps included a winged
Gorgon, a cock, a bronze she-griffin suckling her
young, all witnesses, together with the stadium
itself, to the Greeks' intense interest in life, so con-
trasted with the Egyptian obsession with death.

Throughout the *Altis* are other buildings devoted
to the enhancement of life; exercise-yards, gym-
nasia, hostels, baths and fountains. The design and
the layout change continually. The primary temples
are in the severe Doric style; next we have the
modified Ionic of the Hellenic period, then Roman
versions of both, with the Corinthian added. Finally
there comes the exedra of Herodes Atticus, which
reminds us of nothing so much as Garnier's Second
Empire Paris Opera House. And why not? The
adornment of the classical age of Hellas is designed
to be a wedding-garment, not a shroud. Nowhere
is this lesson more gracefully proclaimed than at
Olympia.

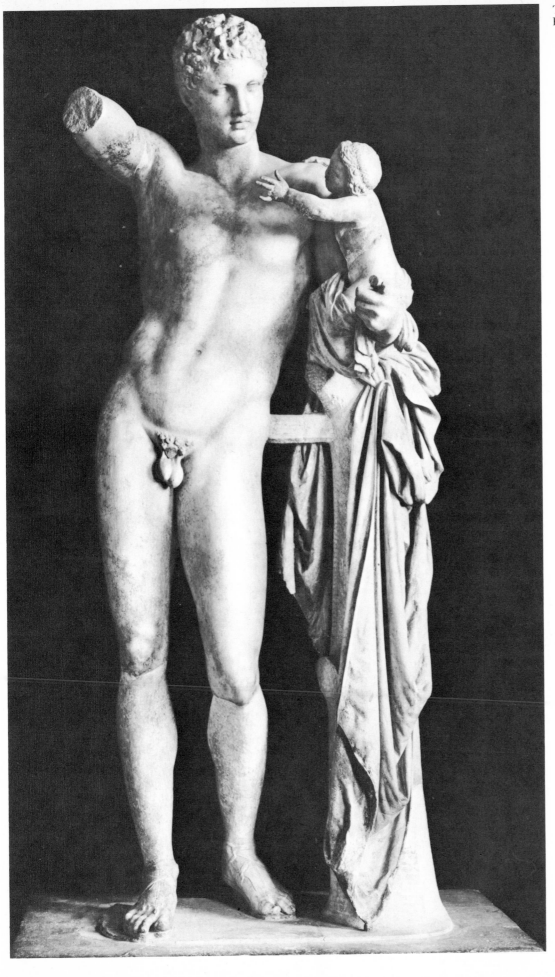

The so-called 'Hermes of Praxiteles'.

# CHAPTER IV

# Corinth

Yes, Olympia was magnificent; its Zeus one of the seven wonders of the world.* But the Games took place during only one month every four years. What were the Greeks doing during the other forty seven months? The answer is what we might expect. They did not spend their time gliding beneath marble porticoes, clad in trailing white robes, discussing philosophy. They were hard at work making a living. Greece is no easy country to live in, or live off. Only on the plains of Boeotia and Thessaly is it possible to establish a viable family-supporting agronomy, which is why from all other parts of Greece save them, the inhabitants from the earliest days until our own have been driven to seek new homes oversea.

As Hegel pointed out, only mountains divide, seas unite. The Aegean was naturally enough a Greek lake from time immemorial; but Hellenes emigrated equally to the north (as the story of the Trojan War reminds us) to the south and to the west. The east was barred, until after the conquests of Alexander the Great, by the powerful empires of Assyria and Babylon, and by the hardy and enterprising Phoenicians, lords of Tyre and Sidon, themselves great seafarers. The northern colonies, which included many in the Black Sea and even in South Russia itself, rich in gold (whence the story of the Golden Fleece) and corn, were little more than trading-posts. The northern climate is too raw for the Greek way of life, which is a predominantly out of doors existence, and is only at home between the isotherms of 5° and 25° centigrade. The earliest European settlement in Africa, in Cyrenaica, was Greek, and by the end of the seventh century the Greeks of Ionia, chiefly Milesians, had established an official 'factory' at Naukratis on the Canopic branch of the Nile. But it was the west that beckoned most clearly, and so numerous were the Greek colonies in southern Italy and Sicily that the region came to be known as 'Magna Graecia'. It was from these colonies that Rome was to draw her first lessons in Hellenism.

In this enterprise, no city of Hellas was to have a greater and more impressive share than Corinth, which is only one of the reasons, though one of the most important, why Corinth was to play a predominant role in the fortunes of both Hellas and Rome.

As a colonization centre Corinth was uniquely favoured. Not only did it lie on the land route which joins northern and southern Hellas, but it possessed not one port but two, Cenchrea on the east and Lechaeum on the west. This twofold outlook is reflected in the great temple of Apollo, which alone of Doric temples had a vestibule at the west end as well as at the east.

Not only geography promoted Corinth. It had two further assets. It was the site of a copious perennial spring, as it still is, the famous Peirene. Throughout the Mediterranean and the Levant springs are rare, which is why they are accounted holy. The spring of Peirene was believed to owe its origin to Pegasus, the winged horse of the hero Bellerophon, from whose hoof as it touched the earth of Corinth the fountain welled up. Pegasus became the patron of Corinth, as well he might, and appears on the city's silver coins. The water of Peirene was believed to give a special quality to one of the city's chief exports, namely its bronze. This was accounted the best type of bronze, perhaps because, as Pausanias tells us, it was annealed in the waters of the famous spring.

For the reason already given on page 10 ancient bronze – whether statues, vessels or mere rivets was in great demand by them, and tons of it found its way into the crucible. Which may well lead us to suppose that bronze objects were much rarer in the ancient world than in fact they were. Corinthian bronze was specially prized. It is even said that the famous Corinthian capital (of which the earliest known example is the now vanished one from Bassae) may have had a metal original. The Greeks had a pretty story about it. A Corinthian maiden, betrothed to a

*The other six were the Pyramids, the Mausoleum at Halicarnassus, the Hanging Gardens of Babylon, the Temple of Artemis at Ephesus, the Colossus of Rhodes and the Pharos (lighthouse) of Alexandria.

*Opposite*
Corinth's most splendid colony was at Syracuse, in Sicily, founded about 734 BC. The temple of Athena was built in the early fifth century and its ruins were incorporated into the Christian cathedral centuries later. It is thus the only Doric temple still used as a place of worship.

SENATVS
POPVLVSQVEROMANVS
DIVOTITODIVIVESPASIANI F
VESPASIANOAVGVSTO

The combination of the Corinthian capital with the older Ionic produced the 'composite' capital, much in favour with the Romans. Here, on the Arch of Titus (AD 80) are some of the earliest surviving examples.

handsome lover, died in the autumn before they could we wed. Her old nurse collected all her little trinkets and put them in a round metal box. This she deposited on top of the maiden's tomb. Next spring, a Corinthian, passing the low mound, was amazed to see that a fine acanthus plant had grown up from below the box and had spread its beautiful shiny leaves all around it. He at once reported his find to the coppersmiths of Corinth, who saw in this touching souvenir the model for a new art-form, the Corinthian capital. That it may have had a metallic origin is supported by Vitruvius, the great Roman authority on architecture, who says the capital was invented by Callimachus at Corinth. Pausanias tells us that Callimachus fashioned a golden lamp for Athens in the Erechtheium. Pliny

says that the portico built at Rome by Gneius Octavius was called Corinthian from its bronze Corinthian capitals. Callimachus was a sculptor, and was the first to use the running drill. We may therefore confidently, with Fr Levi, account him the inventor of the Corinthian capital. He flourished in the latter half of the fifth century BC.

Besides its bronze trade, Corinth was also famous for its pottery. This was exported far and wide. The influence of oriental patterns, such as those of textiles and carpets, is plainly discernible in many of its designs.

The colonies of Greece were never provinces of the 'metropolis' or mother-city, nor did they resemble Roman colonies which were privileged expatriate Romes from Rome. When a Greek colonial enterprise was to be launched, the oracle at Delphi was usually consulted as to the site, and the founding fathers then went forth headed by a leader called the *oikistes*, or founder. The deities of the homeland would be venerated by the new settlement, and formal visits would be exchanged by ambassadors for great feasts. The relationship between home and colony was a family one, like that between parent and grown-up child. If the colony in its turn wanted to found an offshoot, it asked for an *oikistes* from the original mother-city. The only exception to this mother-daughter relationship was that of Corinth and her overseas settlements. As a stepping-stone to Sicily, and Syracuse, Corinth had planted a colony at Corcyra (Corfu). Corinth tried to keep her dependent. This according to Thucydides led to 'the earliest Greek naval battle', traditionally dated 664 BC, and provoked a feud. The Corcyreans claimed that 'colonists are not sent out to be subjects, but to be equals', thereby stating the accepted Greek doctrine of colonial status, the status which was to be re-affirmed more than two thousand years later by the Britons of North America. Later on, Corinth did establish a kind of empire over her colonies in north-west Greece. That was in the seventh century also, two hundred years before Athens attempted the same thing.

Sicily provided the ideal setting for Greek colonization, and of the many settlements – there were thirteen, nearly all on the coasts – Syracuse, Corinth's foundation, easily attained the primacy. So prosperous and powerful did it become that it rose to be the most important city not only in Sicily but in the whole western world. Poets and dramatists went there, including Simonides and Bacchylides; Pindar wrote some of his odes there, and described Syracuse as the 'queen of all cities'. Aeschylus saw his own plays presented in the theatre there; Euripides visited the city, and his dramas were favourites with the Syracusan élite. In the year 480 BC the Syracusans defeated the Carthaginians at the sea-battle of Himera, fought on the same day, it was related, as the battle of Salamis, thus making the Mediterranean world safe for Hellenism in west and east alike. As a thank-offering for this victory, the ruler of Syracuse dedicated a temple to Athena. It is incorporated in the cathedral, and is the only Doric temple still used as a place of worship.

In the mid-fourth century Corinth more than made amends for any harshness she had shewn her daughter. A period of ruinous internecine strife was terminated by the intervention of a Corinthian called Timoleon, sent out at the request of the Syracusans. So complete was his success that the grateful citizens bade him stay on among them, and when he died erected a memorial to him, near the modern Piazza Marconi. He has justly been compared with Augustus and George Washington.

With the development of Athenian imperialism, the rivalry between Athens and Corinth became acute. Athenian interference in the affairs of Megara, half-way between Athens and Corinth, exasperated the Corinthians; and it was disputes over Corcyra and Potidaea, another Corinthian colony on the trade-route to Macedonia, that led to the Pelopon-

nesian War in 431. In this deplorable inter-Hellenic strife Corinth lost heavily in ships, trade and colonies; but it was the Corinthians under the Spartan Gylippus who were largely responsible for the defeat of the Athenians in the disastrous siege of Syracuse in 413, which forever broke Athenian domination.

After the battle of Chaeronea in 338, at which Philip of Macedon extinguished Greek independence, Corinth became the capital of the new Hellenic League and headquarters of the campaign against Persia; and in the post-Alexandrine world it outstripped Athens as the chief centre of commerce, industry and above all of pleasure. On the great citadel above the city, the Akrocorinth, in a precinct dedicated to Aphrodite, no less than one thousand prostitutes followed their calling, and Pindar praised a young man who had munificently augmented their number.

The shadow of Rome was now drawing across the Hellenic world like an eclipse. In the year 196, after the final overthrow of Macedon, the philhellene Roman general Flamininus declared that Greece was to be free, and it was on the isthmus of Corinth, not in Athens, that he made his declaration. But alas for freedom: the Greeks had forgotten how to use it. They foolishly revolted against Rome, and so the Roman general Mummius utterly destroyed

Portrait head of Faustina the Younger, who died in AD 175, from a site near the south Stoa of Corinth. She was the wife of Marcus Aurelius.

*Opposite*
Peirene – the sacred spring as
it appears today.

Corinth in 146. By express order of the Senate, the
city was burned to the ground. Mummius presented
twenty gilded shields to the sanctuary at Olympia,
but despite that gesture looted Corinth ruthlessly,
and many a treasure was stolen or destroyed. Only
the old temple was spared. Of this seven columns
still stand today, among the most often photographed pillars in the world, and two others lie on
the ground, on which may be described traces of
the Greek stucco and Roman plaster which once
covered them. These columns are the only survivors
of one of the oldest temples in Greece, of the Doric
order, archaic of the sixth century. Such forlorn
relics have a fascination, a human appeal which the
regular and regulated precision of the 'classical',
that is mathematical, structure does not possess.

Corinth lay desolate for just a century. A friend
of Cicero's, writing to him in the year 45, says;
'On my return from Asia, I was sailing from Aegina
towards Megara, and began to look at the regions
about me. Behind me was Aegina, in front Megara,
Piraeus to the right, Corinth to the left, all at one

time flourishing towns, now lying prostrate and in
ashes before my eyes.' To such abject ruin had
Rome brought Greece. But the very next year,
Corinth was to rise again. Just before his death,
Julius Caesar refounded Corinth as the capital of
the province of Achaia.

This action of Caesar produced two results which
he never foresaw. The first is that his new city was
to be the setting for some of the most vivid scenes
in the life of Saint Paul; and the second is that
here in Corinth, as nowhere else, we possess a
Greek city which is wholly, with the exception of
the temple, a Roman creation.

Paul arrived in Corinth from Athens in the course
of his second missionary journey in or about the
year 50 AD. He lived there for eighteen fruitful
months, or perhaps longer; and it was in Corinth
that he wrote the earliest document of the New
Testament, namely his first letter to the brethren
of Thessalonika. As usual Paul encountered opposition. The orthodox Jews were naturally perturbed
by this co-religionist of theirs who seemed to preach
heresy. He was also a Roman citizen, that is in the
eyes of the more devout practically a 'collaborator'
with the pagan oppressor. In the year 51 or 52
there came a new governor to the province of Achaia,
a cultivated Roman of Spanish extraction called
Gallio, brother of the famous philosopher and play-
wright Seneca, the tutor of Nero, who succeeded to
the purple in 54. The godly therefore haled Paul
before the tribune, and accused him to Gallio.
Gallio refused to be drawn into what he regarded
as a purely communal difference of opinion; whereupon the Greeks, taking their cue from the governor,
seized the ruler of the synagogue and thrashed him.
Gallio took no notice. (*Acts* XVIII. 12 et seq.)

The episode is of great value as shewing the
attitude of a Roman proconsul towards the
squabbles, as saw them, of oriental inferiors. He
could not have known that of all the many religions
that flourished in that motley province in his day,
the only two which would flourish two thousand
years later were those of the two contestants in this
very case, that of Paul and that of his accusers.

The restored city is described by Pausanias, and
we today, thanks to the excavations carried out by
American enterprise and skill since 1896, can enter
into its life as we can very seldom elsewhere. Outside the Museum there is a range of capitals which
demonstrates the development and perfecting of the
famous Corinthian, beloved by the Romans beyond
all others for its air of opulence. Combined with the
Ionic it produced the composite capital, one of the
earliest examples of which adorns the arch of Titus
at Rome.

As in other Greek cities, the Agora was the heart
and centre. That of Corinth is larger than the Roman
Forum. We can still approach it along the remains
of the sumptuous colonnaded, marble-paved way
which led up from Lechaeum, Corinth's western
port. This creation, like so much Roman architecture, was meant to impress; and how it must have
succeeded, leading up as it did to a triumphal arch,
surmounted by the chariots of Apollo and his son
Phaëthon in gilded bronze, which gave access to the

St Paul made a dramatic
appearance before Gallio,
brother of Seneca, when he
was governor of Achaia in the
year AD 51. This is the earliest
known portrait of him, of the
eighth century, in Santa
Maria Antiqua, Rome.

Agora itself. The colonnade was flanked by a basilica, or lawcourt and assembly hall, with a nave and two side aisles – which the first Christians adopted as the model for their churches. Corinth possessed two other basilicas, on the east and south sides of the Agora. The main basilica was enlarged in the second century AD, owing to the ever-growing commercial prosperity of the city, and equipped with a false façade, adorned with colossal figures of barbarians standing on bases carved with representations of Roman victories.

The Agora is flanked by two rows of shops. That on the south, nearest the Acrocorinth, is the longest colonnade we know of in Greece. Beneath it is a canal of running water. A vertical shaft from each shop provided a space above this canal for hanging perishables such as fresh meat and vegetables, the cool current generated by the water acting as a refrigerator. Or perhaps it was employed to cool wine: scores of broken beakers have been recovered

from the wells.

In front of the colonnade stood the *Bema* or tribune, itself flanked by more shops. The foundations of the *Bema* are clearly discernible. Here we can stand in the very place where Paul stood and can recreate for ourselves the very scene in which he was the protagonist. Jutting into the Agora on the north side the Romans overlooked (because it had been built over before 146 BC) a little oracular shrine, decorated with triglyphs. One of the triglyphs was hinged, and gave access to a sacred spring. A concealed hierophant could thence deliver apparently supernatural utterances, and the spring might on occasion run with wine instead of water.

The theatre lies north-west of the Agora. It could seat 18,000 spectators. About the year AD 135 it was rebuilt in marble, and in the next century it was remodelled to accommodate not only water ballets but also the gladiatorial exhibitions so dear to the coarse Roman heart. An inscription tells the familiar

story of the gladiator Androcles who was spared by a lion from whose paw he had once extracted a thorn. Near the theatre is an Odeum, or concert-hall, which held about 3,000.

In a city given to such amusements we should hardly expect to find a stadium, outdoor athletics being no longer in fashion. The old Greek city had one, and its starting lines can still be seen at the east end of the Agora, which the Romans simply dumped on the area which the stadium had formerly occupied.

Apart from the main public buildings dating from the Caesarian foundation there is one of rare beauty, the fountain-house provided for the spring of Pirene by Herodes Atticus, the millionaire friend of the emperor Hadrian. It is typical of its age, constructed of fluent curves, apses and contrasting planes of light and shade, a masterpiece of that manipulation of space in which Roman construction of the imperial golden age has never been surpassed.

There were plenty of springs in the town, and so a number of baths; but Hadrian presented another, and supplied it with water brought by an aqueduct from Lake Stymphalus thirty miles to the south-west.

The splendid collections of ceramics, of bronzes and of marble statues in the Museum can give us some idea of what the city looked like in the hey-day of the Roman empire, when monuments of gilded bronze, of gold, of ivory and precious stones glittered on every hand, and Corinth was the masque of Hellas the world's pleasure-dome. A magnificent and thrilling picture of this glamorous, clamorous city at the summit of its ease and fame is given by Apuleius who in his *Golden Ass* describes the sumptuous and yet satirical procession to the sea and back in honour of the goddess Isis, as it was performed in Corinth in the days of Marcus Aurelius.

'Not everyone is lucky enough to go to Corinth,' wrote Horace, Rome's most charming Epicurean. The fascination of Corinth for us is that it is Greece as Rome imagined Greece to be, and was unsparing in its striving to reconstruct it as such. Of all the surviving imperial portrait heads in the Museum which include Augustus and his grandson Lucius, none is more revealing than that of Nero, as a young philhellene of twenty years. On his tour of Greece, he visited neither Athens nor Sparta. He made Corinth his headquarters. Here, like Flamininus before him, he proclaimed the freedom of Hellas and competed in the Isthmian games. He even started to dig the Corinth canal, an enterprise not completed until 1893.

Besides being an interpretation Corinth is also a paradox. The city of pleasure, consecrated to the goddess of profane love, was also to call forth the noblest paean to sacred love ever penned; for it was to his flock at Corinth that Paul wrote that 'Now abideth these three, faith, hope and love, but the greatest of these is love.'

51

# CHAPTER V
# Realms of Gold

Corinth shewed Hellas what the Romans thought Hellas should be. Pursuing his perambulations southward, Pausanias came to Argos, and to the country which not only to the Roman masters of Greece but to the Greeks themselves was largely *terra incognita*. Here, if anywhere in Greece, we may feel superior; we can contemplate and understand a Greece that the Greeks knew only by report, through the haze of legend. This epiphany we owe to one man – Heinrich Schliemann.

It is given to few men either to make myth a reality or to make reality a myth. Heinrich Schliemann did both. To quote Ceram: 'Now comes a fairy-tale, the story of the poor boy who at the age of seven dreamed of finding a city, and who thirty-nine years later went forth, sought, and found not only the city but also treasure such as the world had not seen since the loot of the Conquistadores.'

'The fairy-tale is the life of Heinrich Schliemann, one of the most astounding personalities not only among archaeologists but among all men to whom any science has ever been indebted.'

It is to this one man that we owe the recovery both of Troy and of Mycenae, the twin poles of an age. Troy lies above the Dardanelles, near Byzantium, Mycenae in the region of Argos, 250 miles to the south-west; but it was from Mycenae that the leader of the great expedition against Troy arose, from Mycenae 'rich in gold', and that leader's name was Agamemnon. The *Iliad* of Homer, the oldest poem in the Greek tongue, the Bible of the Greeks, tells the tale of Troy. The fate of Agamemnon, murdered on his return by his faithless wife Klytemnestra, is one of the oldest themes in Greek tragic drama. For the Greeks history began with Troy.

The Romans in their turn venerated Troy. The poet Horace realized that it must have been very old, even in Agamemnon's day:

*Vixere fortes ante Agamemnona*

he sang. 'Valiant heroes there were before Agamemnon, many a one. But all of them, unwept, unknown are beset by the long night, because they

lacked an inspired poet,' such as Homer – or Horace; that is they were pre-Homeric. In Horace's day, no one doubted that Troy had been a real city. Herodotus had told them that Xerxes once visited New Ilion to contemplate the remains of Priam's fortress and to sacrifice a thousand cattle to Athena of Ilion. Xenophon relates that Mindarus, the Spartan admiral, had done the same. Alexander as usual went one better. He not only sacrificed there, but took some weapons away with him and bade his bodyguard carry them in battle for luck. Julius Caesar embellished New Ilion, partly out of piety, and also because the Romans, in order to feel 'as good as' the Greeks had by this time adopted the notion that they were descended from Trojan Aeneas, an idea that Virgil was to consecrate in his epic.

Had all these eminent people been misled by a fiction? At the beginning of the nineteenth century it was generally held that they had been, that Troy was a beautiful myth. A seven-year-old German boy thought otherwise. In the year 1829, Heinrich Schliemann, son of a Lutheran pastor in Neu Buckow, an abscure township of Mecklenburg-Schwerin in northern Germany, was given as a Christmas present by his father Jerrer's *Illustrated History of the World*, which contained a picture of Aeneas leading his son Iulus by the hand, with his old father Anchises on his back, as they fled from the burning citadel of Troy. Shakespeare knew the story (*Julius Caesar*, Act I, Scene 2, lines 112–14); Raphael had made the scene famous in a fresco in the Vatican. 'Is that how Troy looked?' asked the lad. His father nodded. 'And is it all gone and nobody knows where it stood?' 'That is true,' replied his father. 'I don't believe that,' said Heinrich. 'When I'm grown up I shall go to Greece and find Troy and the king's treasure.'

Thirty-nine years later he did just that. His sensible father nourished his son's interest in antiquity. In 1832 when Heinrich was ten, his Christmas present was a book about the Trojan War. 'Little did I think,' wrote Schliemann 'that thirty-six years later I should offer the public a book on the same subject. And to do this moreover after actually

*Above*
Heinrich Schliemann, 1822–1800.
*Opposite*
Sophia Schliemann wearing the jewels of Troy.

The Palace of Nestor at Pylos. In the foreground can be seen the foundations of the gate tower and, to the left, the archive room where 600 Linear B tablets were found. The palace was built about 1300 BC.

seeing with my own eyes the scene of the fatherland and the heroes immortalized by Homer.'

The idea that Schliemann was a 'gifted amateur' is quite wrong. He was a natural-born scholar with an amazing talent for languages, although it took him a year or so to realize it. At fourteen he had to start to earn his living, which he did as an apprentice in a grocer's shop in Fürstenberg. For five years he sold herrings, brandy, milk and salt. He crushed potatoes to make spirit with, he swept out the shop. He toiled from five in the morning until eleven at night. One day a drunken mill-hand came into the

shop and started to recite. Heinrich understood not a word; but when he discovered that the poor sot was reciting from the *Iliad* he bought him a schnapps, and had him recite the verses all over again.

In 1841 Heinrich signed on as a cabin-boy in a ship bound for Venezuela; the ship was wrecked off the Dutch island of Texel but he survived, and became an office-boy in Amsterdam. There he started to learn his languages. He reckoned that it took him six weeks to learn a language, and within two years he has mastered English, French, Dutch,

A contemporary sketch of Schliemann's excavations in the Troad, 1870. The site shown was believed to be that of the Scaean Gate and the Palace of Priam.

'It was not until 1854 that I was able to learn Swedish and Polish,' he writes blandly. In 1850, he went from Russia to the United States of America. He was in California when that territory was admitted to the Union, and so automatically became an American citizen (his certificate of naturalization is preserved in the Gennadion at Athens). He set up a bank for dealing in gold. He called on President Taylor, or perhaps it was Fillmore. This Mecklenburger of twenty-eight and the President chatted for an hour and a half.

Schliemann next visited Egypt, Palestine, Syria and Greece, a journey on which he learned Latin and Arabic. In 1864 he went around the world and wrote his first book, about Japan, in French. He was now rich, 'far beyond my ambitious expectations'.

'I retired from business,' he said, 'so that I could devote myself entirely to the studies that so completely fascinated me.' But he remained as proud of his mercantile acumen as he was of his archaeological lore. When applying to the University of Rostock for a doctor's degree he wrote an account of his tycoon's career in classical Greek. He obtained his doctorate.

Now at last he was ready for his destiny, this sorcerer-apprentice, Merchant of the Imperial Guild of St Petersburg, Judge of the St Petersburg Imperial Court, director of the Imperial State Bank. In 1868 he set out for Ithaca, which he had been prevented from visiting by illness during his visit to Greece in 1859.

Ithaca is an identifiable island. Edward Lear had been there five years before and depicted it in delicate watercolours. But Troy? No one knew where it was, if indeed it was anywhere. Most supposed it to be a dream-city, a myth. The story of the *Iliad* begins with 'far-darting Apollo' sending a pestilence among the Achaeans. Zeus himself watches the struggle from Mount Ida; Poseidon is

Spanish, Portuguese and Italian. In 1844 he began to study Russian.

His method was to carry on imaginary conversations out loud—a method which twice led to his being asked to find other lodgings. Schliemann did well in the Amsterdam merchant house and at the age of twenty-four he went to St Petersburg as their agent. In 1847 he founded his own import-export business in that city, opened a second branch in Moscow in 1852, and so was admirably placed to make a fortune out of the Crimean War, which he duly did.

Tiryns. The courtyard of the
citadel.

perched on Samothrace. Is this history? Of course not. Besides, the world of Homer is the setting for a highly cultivated civilization. Lordly men and women are arrayed in purple and fine linen; they live their lives in stately dwellings with polished walls and floors. Their arms and armour are exquisitely wrought, their womenfolk glitter with golden jewellery, whereas the Greeks, when first they enter history, are a simple folk, few in numbers. They know no great kings, they man no great fleets. It was therefore logical in Schliemann's day to believe that Homer and his world were mythical. For a society still dominated by Winckelmannship, history began with the long process that led up from the archaic embryo to the classical perfection, as the Panathenaic way leads from the Dipylon Gate to the Akropolis.

Schliemann refused to be logical. If not only Herodotus but Thucydides himself had accepted the Trojan War as an actual event, and its protagonists as actual persons, were not Greece's own historians to be given credit for knowing what they were writing about? Thus in 1868 at the age of forty-six this eccentric, but extremely erudite, millionaire set out for Ithaca, the Peloponnese and the Troad. What a fair omen it was that almost the first indigenous Greek he got to know was an Ithacan blacksmith whose wife was called Penelope, and his sons, Odysseus and Telemachus. He read the twenty-third book of the *Odyssey* to the villagers one evening. Overcome with emotion he cried, and the villagers with him, though it is unlikely that they understood a word of so antique a tongue, pronounced in so outlandish an accent – or had Schliemann already mastered the Ithacan dialect?

It was harder for Schliemann's contemporaries to accept his notions that it is for us. Before 1952 it was believed that there had been a gap, more or less complete, between the Homeric culture which had come to an end in the twelfth century BC, and the

Hissarlik, the site of Troy, as it appears today.

The huge fortification walls of the citadel at Tiryns are pierced by corbel-vaulted casemates which were used to store food and weapons in time of siege, and also carried staircases from one level to another. This one led to the postern gate.

*Opposite*
Mycenae, *c.* 1350 BC. The massive lintel measures fifteen feet in length: it is six and a half feet wide and three and a quarter feet high in the centre. The device above is apparently heraldic: similar devices appear on Mycenaean seals.

to the way they say it: it is now clear that there was no break in language between the pre-Homeric and post-Homeric tongue of Hellas. From the fifteenth century BC until our own day this same language has endured, a phenomenon unique in linguistic history. (The first Chinese dictionary, containing 40,000 characters, appeared about 1100 BC. The beginnings of the Semitic alphabet can be traced to about 1860 BC, but not the birth of Hebrew. This may be placed about 1100 BC, but it differs from the earlier Semitic. For a fuller note on 'Linear B', see Chapter VI).

In the absence of such knowledge as we now possess, Schliemann's confidence is all the more remarkable. Those few who admitted that Troy had existed sought its site on a hill called Pinarbaşi, because it is written in the *Iliad* (XXII, 147–52): 'And they came to the two fair-flowing springs, where two fountains rise that feed the deep eddying Skamandros. The one floweth with warm water, and smoke goeth up therefrom around it as it were from a blazing fire, while the other even in summer floweth forth like cold hail or snow or ice that water formeth.'

Schliemann went out to inspect it. 'I admit,' he wrote, 'that I could scarcely control my emotion when I saw the tremendous plain of Troy spread out before me, a scene that had haunted my earliest child-hood dreams.' But he was soon convinced that it was not the site of Troy. For one thing, Pinarbaşi contained not two springs but forty, which gave the place its name. Secondly the knoll was too cramped to have accommodated Priam's palace of sixty-two rooms. Thirdly there was not a trace of ruins on the mound; and lastly, with his watch in one hand and Homer in the other, Schliemann worked out that if Pinarbaşi were Troy, the Achaeans would have had to cover at least fifty-two miles during the first nine hours of battle.

Two and a half hours north from Pinarbaşi and only one hour from the coast stood New Ilion, now called Hissarlik. There were plenty of ruins there. Schliemann was convinced that this really was Troy. The Plain of Troy had for more than two centuries – in fact ever since the establishment of diplomatic relations between Queen Elizabeth I and the Sultan Murad III in 1580 – been investigated by classically-mined travellers of many nations. Byron, who was there for seventeen days in 1810 described it as 'a fine field for conjecture and snipe shooting'. When Schliemann arrived at Hissarlik, he met an English-man who was so convinced that this very mound was ancient Troy that he had bought nearly half of it and had started to dig thereon in 1865. His name was Frank Calvert, one of a family of brothers with antiquarian interests, whose parents and grand-parents seem to have been settled in the region. Frank Calvert acted as British Consul in the Dardanelles at various times between 1887 and 1890, and was American consul for many years. He was familiar with the entire countryside. In Cook's words: 'He deserves much of the credit for the discovery of Troy.'

Schliemann very sensibly consulted Calvert. One thing that puzzled him was the absence of springs:

Greek which, in its archaic form, had started in the eighth. But in 1952 a young Englishman called Michael Ventris, helped by a fellow-countryman called John Chadwick, succeeded in deciphering a number of clay tablets written in a script which Evans had styled 'Linear B'. Three thousand of these tablets had been found in Knossos. In 1939 the American archaeologist Blegen found 600 more in the palace of Nestor at Pylos in south-west Greece. In the early fifties Wace found fifty at Mycenae. Since then 'Linear B' tablets have come to light in places as far north as Thebes in Boeotia.

In 1952 the great discovery was made. These tablets, pictographic – that is pre-alphabetic – though they be, are nevertheless written in Greek, a primitive form of the language admittedly, but still unmistakably Greek. The contents of the tablets are commonplace, they are tallies and records, not written for all time nor even for an age, mere book-keeping entries. But what they say is as nothing

there was no sign of them. Calvert explained, quite correctly, that seismic disturbance constantly alters the output of springs in this region, or even chokes them altogether. Schliemann accepted this explanation. He was moreover persuaded that the running fight between Hector and Achilles was feasible in the terrain of Hissarlik, with its gentle incline, whereas at Pinarbaşi, with a precipitate cleft to negotiate, it would have been impossible.

In his *Ithaka, der Peloponnes und Troja*, completed on the last day of 1868, Schliemann propounded two theories: (a) Hissarlik and not Pinarbaşi was the site of Troy, and (b) at Mycenae the graves of the Atreidae were not outside the walls (where ancient graves were normally sited) but inside them, as Pausanias says. Pausanias' words (Book II, xvi) are: 'In the ruins of Mycenae. . . . There is the grave of Atreus and the graves of those who came home from Troy, to be cut down by Aegisthus at his supper party.' Agamemnon and Kassandra were among those who came home from Troy, and Aegisthus was in love with Agamemnon's queen, Klytemnestra. Pausanias goes on: 'Klytemnestra and Aegisthus were buried a little further from the wall. They were not fit to lie inside' (the city) 'where Agamemnon and the men murdered with him are lying.' (Fr Levi's translation). On both these points Schliemann was to be proved, or rather was to prove himself, right.

Schliemann's first wife, after bearing him three children, had found herself unable to share what was in her view a vagabond existence. In 1869 therefore he married a Greek girl called Sophia Engastromenos, whom he had acquired unromantically enough by postal enquiry. Sophia turned out to be as devoted and skilful as she was beautiful, and was of invaluable help to Heinrich on his explorations.

These started at Troy in 1870. Schliemann burrowed with relentless determination, destroying in the process much valuable evidence. Down, down he went, encountering walls, weapons and furnishings, ornaments and vases. Clearly a great city had stood here . . . But not one city only. Wall was piled on wall, floor upon floor. Schliemann was so certain that the original Troy lay at the very bottom that he went right through it without realizing that he had done so. He ended up in a city of the epoch we now call Neolithic, before man had learned the use of metals, that is of about 2,500 BC, more than a thousand years before the age of Homer. But that Troy had existed and that Homer was right – that he had proved. His first report, dated 21 April 1870 is addressed to the president of the Institut de France.

After four arduous seasons Schliemann felt that he had earned a respite. He decided to suspend his operations on 15 June 1873. On the 14th, he came on a treasure that was to dazzle the world. His workmen were twenty feet below the surface. Schliemann was as usual watching from above with his wife beside him. Suddenly his eye caught the glint of gold. At once he bade his wife dismiss the workmen on the pretext that he had forgotten it was his birthday. He then went to work himself at the bottom of the trench, in peril of his life from the impending mass of debris and the citadel wall above him. 'The sight of so many immeasurably priceless objects made me foolhardy and I did not think of hazards.'

The hoard was transferred to Sophia's red shawl. There were brooches, diadems, chains, plaques, buttons, gold wire, bracelets. Not for one moment did Schliemann doubt that he had found the treasure of Priam. Later investigations were to prove, shortly before Schliemann's death, that what he had in fact secured was the treasure of a king who had lived a thousand years before Priam. The whole priceless collection was smuggled out of the country, with the help of Sophia's connections, and so to Athens, and thence finally to Germany. (When Schliemann's house was searched at the insistence of the Turkish ambassador, no trace of gold was found in it). Schliemann used to display some of his finds on his beautiful wife. After his death they were to be seen in Berlin; but since the war they have wholly disappeared. This was only one of nineteen eventual caches of precious objects to be found in Troy, but it has naturally remained the most famous.

Excavations at the grave circle, Mycenae. Sophia Schliemann can be seen in the foreground. A contemporary engraving, 1876.

Schliemann was universally hailed as the re-discoverer of Troy. At fifty-one he had reached a zenith of fame. But not for him rest or retirement. He must now prove the correctness of his second theory, about the burials at Mycenae. This he was shortly to do; but since Mycenae and Troy are so intimately linked, it will be well to round off the tale of Troy before proceeding to the sister site.

The Turkish authorities were incensed, naturally enough, at Schliemann's clandestine *coup*, and it was not until 1878 that they would allow him to resume his work at Troy. This was the immediate cause of his going to Mycenae. In 1878 and the following year he was assisted at Troy by Rudolf Virchow, the great pathologist who in 1856 had declared that the famous 'Neanderthal Man' was the skeleton of a gouty old dotard – an odd companion to choose, it may seem in retrospect. In 1882 Schliemann had a far more profitable assistant, the twenty-nine year old Dörpfeld, who had learned his art at Olympia. Already in 1879 Schliemann had realized that Troy was more complex than he had supposed. In his *Ilios* (1879) he had postulated seven citadels. His *Troja* (1884) is a far better book. Dörpfeld had been able to identify no less than nine superimposed towns. In 1932 Blegen undertook a meticulous re-examination of the site. He worked for seven seasons and his findings largely confirmed Dörpfeld's: Dörpfeld's nine settlements stood up well; but each was broken down into sub-phases so that in the end Troy was

The entrance to the building which Schliemann believed to be a treasury but which was almost certainly a sepulchre. It has been called both the Tomb of Agamemnon and the Treasury of Atreus.

The murder of Agamemnon and Kassandra, and the killing of Klytemnestra and Aegisthus by Agamemnon's son Orestes in revenge, brought the total up to twelve.

Everything in Mycenae and in all the region of Argos is tainted. Athens was said by Pindar to be

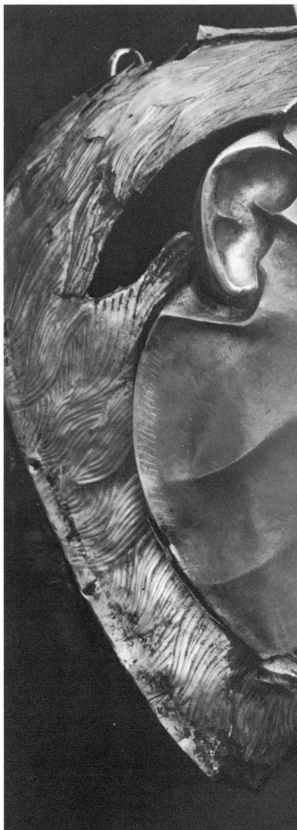

In the so-called Tomb of Clytemnestra. The vault from below.

shewn to be forty-six layers deep. When did Troy fall? Greek literary sources would place the catastrophe in 1184. Nor were they far out: Blegen has established it as having taken place in or about 1240 BC.

At the end of the Trojan War, Agamemnon set out for his home in Mycenae, and Odysseus for his in Ithaca. Odysseus was to be ten years on the journey – but for which we should not have known the delights of Homer's *Odyssey*. Agamemnon announced his impending arrival in Mycenae by a chain of beacons, such as would one day announce the arrival of the Invincible Armada off the coast of England. The first flame blazed on Mount Ida, whence it passed to Lemnis, to Mount Athos, to Euboea, across Boeotia, to Megara and the Saronic Gulf and finally to the mountain above Mycenae itself. (All twelve beacons are named in Aeschylus' *Agamemnon*).

At length Agememnon arrives bringing with him Kassandra, the hapless Trojan princess he has made his concubine. By the time of his return, to meet his death at the hands of his treacherous and unfaithful wife and her paramour Aegisthus, Mycenae had already been the scene of eight horrible murders connected with Pelops and his progeny. John Milton was fascinated by the story. His *Penseroso* dreams:

> Sometime let gorgeous Tragedy
> In sceptred pall come sweeping by,
> Presenting Thebes, or Pelops' line,
> Or the tale of Troy divine.

'god-haunted'. The Argolid is 'guilt-haunted'. It is as though the Greeks, to preserve the brightness of Hellas, had found here a sump, as it were, into which to drain all the impurities of human frailty. Mycenae according to legend was founded by Perseus, who after many adventures settled in nearby Tiryns. Roaming over the hills one day he lost his scabbard-cap (*mykes*) or found a nice mushroom (*mykos*) or perhaps heard the howling of the wind in the rocks (*mykithmos*) which was Schliemann's preference. At a blow from his sword, the spring *Perseis* gushed forth and Perseus founded his city hard by it.

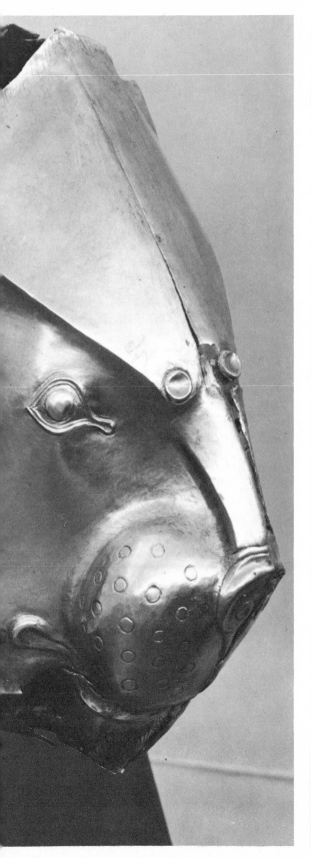

*Far left*
A gold rhyton (funnel-shaped vessel) in the form of a lion's head, from Grave IV, Mycenae. National Museum, Athens.
*Left*
Mycenaean gold-inlaid bronze dagger. National Museum, Athens.

Herakles passed that way, and performed his labours for the then king Eurystheus. These were the 'valiant men' who as Horace sings had lived 'before Agamemnon'. In fact the site had been occupied in the third millenium BC; but the great civilization we still call Mycenean arose in the latter half of the second, in the Period called Late Helladic I, about 1600 BC. It lasted for some five hundred years, and then disappeared. Agamemnon comes into the picture almost at the end of it.

The lords of this sinister citadel, at the apogee of their power, ruled over wider dominions than any Greek state was to command until the unification of Greece in the nineteenth century AD. Subordinate strongholds included Tiryns, Midea, Asine and Hermione. Mycenae held sway over all the Peloponnese; and her cultural influence extended to Attica, Boeotia, Thessaly, Phokis, Ionia and the Aegean islands. Even Crete, which had amply inspired Mycenae, was now subordinated to the daughter kingdom. Trade with Egypt flourished. This great empire left vivid memories to after ages, beginning with the epics of Homer. Troy was remote, and men might be forgiven for losing sight of it; but Mycenae was in the heart of Greece, and gigantic relics of it endured through the ages. Pausanias saw the Lion Gate, and some of the tombs and 'treasure-houses'. The great walls, of massive polyhedronic boulders like those at Tiryns, could only have been piled up, men said, by the Cyclopes, those one-eyed Calibans of antiquity, whence the name 'Cyclopean' for this type of masonry which we still employ. Lord Elgin's roving chaplain, Dr Hunt, proposed to move the Erechtheium to London, but had to admit the impossibility of so transferring the citadel of Mycenae.

What fascinates us about Mycenae today is not only what Pausanias or Dr Hunt beheld but, far more, the vast treasures of which they never even dreamed. And this brings us back to Schliemann.

As we have seen Schliemann had early been attracted to Mycenae. In 1874 he had dug a few trenches there but was, very properly, stopped by the government from whom he had not troubled to ask permission. In the autumn of 1876, duly empowered, he started to dig within the wall, just inside the Lion Gate. The Gate itself stood as it had stood for centuries and as it stands today, the most impressive of all Greek portals and the oldest sculpture in the round in Europe. The two beasts, lionesses probably, form a heraldic achievement. A seal found at Mycenae shews a similar device, with a dove on top of the pillar. Another from Crete – there were no coins in those days, nor for five hundred years later – shews the mother-goddess on a peak flanked by two lionesses. The device may have been a royal badge. Today it is the symbol of the Royal Institute of British Architects.

Almost at once Schliemann found what he was looking for. First he unearthed a quantity of vases, including the famous 'warrior vase' which is now in the National Museum of Athens; this depicts Mycenaean soldiers in their habit, as they were. Then he laid bare a circular structure formed of a double row of stones set on edge. Schliemann, with his quicksilver wit, at once assumed that this was the agora in which the elders sat to do justice and to plan policy. He recalled that Pausanias, in regard to another agora, had written: 'Here they built the place of assembly, in such fashion that the heroes' graves would be in the middle of the meeting-place.' The discovery of nine stelae, four of them with well-preserved bas-reliefs, convinced him that he was standing on Agememnon's grave. He was not: the burials were those of monarchs who had lived

*ante Agamemnona* by four hundred years. That did not matter. Once again Schliemann had proved that Homer was right. Mycenae was no fable.

The treasures which he extracted from the five graves he excavated exceeded in sheer value anything ever brought to light until the discovery of the tomb of Tutankhamun almost half a century later. The Mycenaean Hall in the Athens Museum now houses them, for our astonishment and delight. Even Schliemann was overcome with wonder. He sent ecstatic telegrams to the king of Greece, who was a Dane, congratulating him on the recovery of the mask of his 'ancestor', and to the emperor of Brazil, whom he had entertained at a banquet in the very 'Treasury of Atreus'. He wrote in his beautiful copperplate English hand to Mr Gladstone.

Since Schliemann's day others have followed up his pioneer work at Mycenae, notably the Englishman, A. J. B. Wace. Wace found not only graves but the remains of splendid private houses. He also found the precious Linear B tablets.

Schliemann was convinced that the great *tholos* tombs were treasuries. Nine have been found, and we now know for certain that they were sepulchres, dating from 1520 to 1300 BC. It is just possible that the finest and most famous of them, one of the crowning achievements of all architecture, was indeed the tomb of Agamemnon.

From 1884 to 1886 Schliemann, aided by Dörpfeld, laid bare the citadel of Tiryns, the birthplace of Herakles, whose Cyclopean walls Pausanias compared with the pyramids of Egypt. The palace of Tiryns exceeded in grandeur any found before. The walls at their thickest point are seven or eight yards thick, and in the inner circle where the ruler lived they are eleven yards thick and sixteen yards high. Pausanias may be excused for his comparison.

Schliemann now had a home in Athens, the 'Palace of Troy', just off Syntagma Square, built in 1878. (It now houses the 'Areopagus' or Supreme Court). Baulked of his wish to excavate Knossos, he found himself in Naples in December 1890. He wanted to be back with his wife Sophia and his two children Andromache and Agamemnon for Christmas, but was detained by a harrowing ear ailment. On Christmas Day he collapsed in the Piazza della Santa Carità. He could not speak, but remained conscious. Bystanders took him to a hospital, where he was refused admission; so they left him in a police station. His doctor's address was found in one of his pockets and the doctor was soon on the scene. He could do nothing. Schliemann died the next morning. He was sixty-eight.

When his body was brought to Athens, the King and the Crown Prince, foreign diplomatists, the Greek prime minister and the leaders of the scientific institutes came to pay their last respects. A bust of Homer looked down upon them.

Schliemann had added a thousand years to the immortal record of Greek history. He had recreated for all time what was, in the literal sense of the word, the Golden Age of Hellas.

# Crete—the Dawn of Europe

'Out in the dark blue sea there lies a land called Crete, a rich and lovely land, washed by waves on every side, densely peopled and boasting ninety cities. Each of the several races of the isle has its own language . . .ø thøøtowns is a great city called Knossos, and there, for nine years, King Minos ruled and enjoyed the friendship of almighty Zeus.'

Thus, in Homer's *Odyssey*, Odysseus the wanderer described to his wife Penelope the largest of the Greek islands. It is with the same quotation that Dr Reynold Higgins prefaces his admirable exposition of Crete.

Europe and America had hardly recovered from the shock of Schliemann's relevations, which had added a millenium to recorded time, than they were confronted with another startling addition to the pedigree of civilized man. Just as the great epics were constructed around individual heroes, such as Agamemnon, Achilles and Odysseus, so the recreation of their world was the work of individual genius, first Schliemann and then Evans. Schliemann had started work at Troy at the age of forty-eight, having amassed his own fortune. Arthur Evans started work at Knossos at the age of forty-nine, having inherited his.

He was born in 1851, the son of Sir John Evans, an archaeologist and numismatist of distinction, who had the additional advantage of being a director of the prosperous paper-making firm of John Dickinson. Arthur received as good an education as his father could provide, first at Harrow, then at Brasenose College, Oxford, and finally at Göttingen University. His earliest interest was not in Crete at all, but in the Balkans, an interest which he retained to the end of his days. In 1877 he settled at Ragusa, now Dubrovnik, and when in that year the Serbs rose against the Turks he became the local correspondent of the *Manchester Guardian*. In 1882 he left Ragusa, after seven weeks in prison, having been suspected by the Austrian authorities of complicity in a plot in Herzegovina. Two years later he was appointed keeper of the Ashmolean Museum in Oxford; he reorganized it and brought order into its miscellaneous collections. This post he held until 1908, when his preoccupation with Crete demanded almost his entire attention. He was then appointed Extraordinary Professor of Prehistoric Archaeology in the University of Oxford.

Schliemann had been drawn to Crete, and a year before he died he wrote: 'I should like to crown my career with one great piece of work: namely with the excavation of the extremely old prehistoric palace of Knossos, on Crete, which I believe I discovered three years ago.' that is in 1896; the site of the palace had in fact been discovered in 1878. But even Schliemann could not overcome the local opposition. He had the permission of the governor of Crete, but the man who owned the hill on which the ruins stood would not hear of any 'poking around'. He put a fantastic price on his property. After much haggling the sum asked for was more than halved; but the owner then demanded payment for 2,500 olive trees, which under Ottoman law were normally sold separately from the land on which they grew. Schliemann counted only 888, and so the whole deal was called off. 'For once,' comments Ceram, 'Schliemann's business sense damped his archaeological passion.'

Evans had followed Schliemann's archaeological career with admiring interest. To the end of his days he always, both in private and in public, acknowledged his debt to him. The two men met in Athens in 1882, when Evans and his wife were impressed with Schliemann's ability and scholarship, and amused by what they considered his 'un-English' mannerisms.

Evans' interest in Crete was primarily epigraphical. He paid his first visit to the island in 1894, having acquired in Athens a gem which he thought pointed to Crete. He was sure now that Crete must be his field. As luck would have it, Crete became autonomous in 1898 under a Greek High Commissioner, Prince George, who lived to represent his country at the wedding of Queen Elizabeth and Prince Philip. Evans succeeded in buying the whole site. Thenceforth he was free of all interference, and this fact is important. Evans is sometimes

One side of the celebrated Phaistos disc. It dates from about 1600 BC, is about six inches in diameter and one inch thick. Impressed on both sides with picture-writing like an early form of printing, it remains indecipherable. A running man, a feather headdress, a ship, an eagle, a house and a vase all appear. Though found on a Cretan site, it bears no resemblance to Cretan hieryphic writing.

thought of as a rich man who made Knossos his plaything. Rich he certainly was, but he was also a highly qualified archaeologist and epigraphist by the time he came to Knossos; and if he has been criticised for some of his actions there, it may be remembered that he was simply doing what he liked, and thought right, with his own property. Of how many other sites can this be said?

For forty years, until his death in 1941, Knossos was Evans' one absorbing interest. When he started digging he was forced to admit that he would need at least a twelvemonth to clear the site: twenty-five years later he was still digging on the same spot. Nor is the work yet finished. As his half-sister Joan wrote, 'he had come to the site in hope of finding a seal impression and a clay tablet, and Time and Chance had led him to discover a civilization'.

That is the main difference between Schliemann and Evans. Even those who did not believe in Troy had heard a great deal about it; and there were the citadel of Mycenae and the fortress of Tiryns for all to see. Schliemann had made the stones speak, and had brought to light the treasures of a thousand years. In that sense he had added an epoch to Greek history. Evans was to do more: he would add a whole nation to the tribes of men. He would shew us how they lived their daily lives, what they looked like, what they wore, how they traded and fought, and what games they played. A hitherto unknown people, under Evans' re-creating hand, became a breathing reality.

It must at the outset of even the briefest consideration of Crete be made clear that Evans was not its only investigator, nor Knossos the only Minoan site to yield up its secrets and treasure. At Phaistos, next in size and importance to Knossos, the Italian School of Archaeology in Athens started its work as early as 1900, just when Evans was starting his. The

The so-called Harvester Vase
from Hagia Triada. In fact it
represents a seed-sowing
festival: men carry hoes with
willow-shoots attached to the
ends, while the apparent
leader wears a cloak like a
pine-cone. Four singers and a
dancer accompany the
procession. It dates from
about 1450 BC.

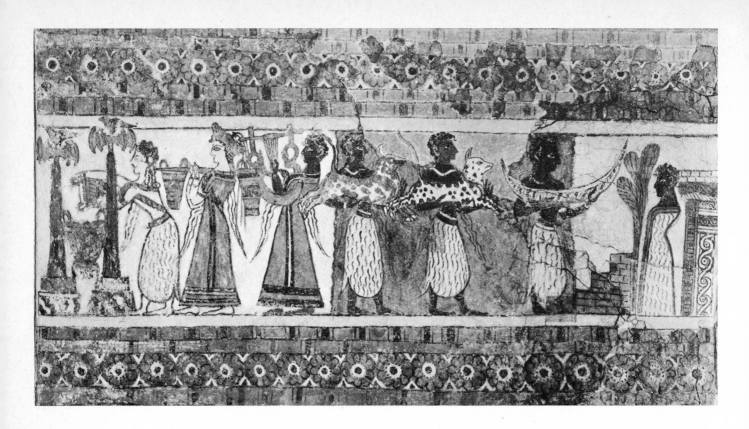

A limestone sarcophagus, painted in fresco technique, from a chamber-tomb near the palace of Hagia Triada. Late Minoan III, from about 1400 BC. Offerings are being brought for the dead man, who stands outside his tomb on the right.

Phaistos disc (1908) is only the most famous of their finds. At Hagia Triada nearby the Italians brought to light the 'harvester vase', the fresco of a cat stalking an unsuspecting pheasant, and a cache of nineteen copper ingots. All these are now in the Herakleion Museum. Finest of all is the painted sarcophagus, which can be seen in the museum's upper storey. At Mallia the French School at Athens has carried on work since 1921. It was at Mallia that the famous golden 'bee-pendant' was found. At Gournia (2000–1300 BC), first described by Evans in 1896, an American expedition uncovered the town during the years 1901–1905, led by the indomitable Miss Harriet Ann Boyd. Nearly three-quarters of a century later it is still the *only* Bronze Age town in the Aegean area to be completely excavated. Naturally enough, Evans' work at Knossos, with its international exhibition atmosphere and extensive publicity, has tended to overshadow these other expeditions, important as they are.

Crete was the home of abundant legend. Zeus himself was said to have been born there, on Mount Ida, of Rhea, wife and sister of Kronos (Crete, like the Troad, has a mountain of that name). He was suckled by a goat called Amalthea. The nymphs tended him and a band of youths protected him from his child-eating father, Kronos. Minos, son of Zeus and Europa, ruled Crete; Minos the terrible, who to settle a private feud invaded Athens and demanded a tribute of seven lads and seven maidens to be sent to Crete every nine years. There, it was rumoured, they were kept in a terrible prison, like a maze, the lair of the Minotaur. This monster was the fruit of Queen Pasiphaë's lust for a bull, sent by Poseidon from the sea as a sacrificial gift to Minos, who found it so handsome that he kept it as a pet.

It was Daedalus the cunning artificer from Athens, who disguised Pasiphaë as a cow to help her to gain her shameful end. He also made the maze, which was called a 'labyrinth' a word connected with the Greek, or rather pre-Greek, word meaning a double-headed axe. This was a sacred symbol in Crete, as so many representations of it abundantly show. Daedalus had also, as we know from Homer, built a dancing-floor for Ariadne, Minos' daughter. Young prince Theseus of Athens, already renowned for his gallantry and bravery, was determined to put an end to Minos' aggressions. So when it came to the third tribute, he himself went as one of the youths. Ariadne fell in love with him, and provided him with the famous thread (another of Daedalus' creations), so that after killing the Minotaur he could make a speedy escape, and Ariadne with him. Daedalus thought it prudent to leave Knossos as well; and so he went by air to Athens, using wings of his own invention. His son, Icarus, flew too near the sun, which melted his wax-fashioned wings. He crashed into the sea and was drowned. Thanks to Brueghel and others his melancholy end has made him far better known than his gifted father: and yet it was Daedalus, who apart from his other achievements, first gave motion to statues by separating their feet.

All this complicated, and indeed confused, story (and only a bare outline or two is here repeated) adds up to far more than a jumble of myths, such as one would find by browsing in a dictionary of mythology. They seem to emerge from a folk-memory of something which really did happen, just as the Homeric legend was proved by Schliemann to be. It was Evans – who called his charming dwelling at Knossos 'Villa Ariadne' – who supplied the thread. What can we reasonably conjecture to have been the substratum of fact. Perhaps something like the following?

In the neolithic epoch, about 6000 BC according to a recent carbon-date from Knossos, a people who may have come from Anatolia settled in Knossos. How long they remained there, and how numerous they became, may be gauged from the fact that of the thirty-eight feet of debris which Evans found beneath the west court of the palace, as we now have it, twenty-four belonged to this settlement. Having no metals, they used tools of stone and obsidian, which is found in Melos and Naxos. Houses were rectangular, an advance on the earlier 'tukul' type found in primitive Jericho. Small rooms clustered around a main one: already we have the plan which would be expanded into the 'palace' design.

In 3000 BC the Minoan Period begins, with the influx of a new people, come from nobody yet knows where. This Minoan Period will last until 1100 BC. Evans divided it into Early Minoan, Middle Minoan and Late Minoan, and each of these epochs was subdivided into three, making nine distinguishable periods in all.

Many new sites are occupied, three distinct pottery styles are found, and copper gradually replaces stone for artefacts. By 'EM II' leaf-shaped copper daggers are common, houses are more complex, and fine jewellery occurs: a lens found at Knossos might be a magnifying glass used by an artist in intaglio. The best architectural survival of this age is the vault beneath the south porch of the palace.

About 2000 BC came the transition from Early to Middle Minoan, marked by wheel-made pottery, notably the so-called Kamares ware, a charming polychrome creation first found in the Kamares cave (4,985 feet) on Mount Ida. Palaces now appear not only at Knossos, but at Mallia and Phaistos. Burial in the great jars, *pithoi*, is introduced. Trade flourishes: Egyptian scarabs are found in Crete, and Cretan pottery in Egypt and the Levant.

In 1700 BC a great catastrophe, probably an earthquake, obliterates all this prosperity. Thereafter the palaces were rebuilt, and the island reached its zenith of felicity, starting with the epoch known as MM IIb. This age lasted nearly eight hundred years, a span of dominion so far exceeded only by Byzantium and Venice, each of which can claim a millennium.

This gave us the Knossos we know, or that Sir Arthur Evans thought we should know. The frescoes, the gay scarlet tapering pillars, the great storage-jars, the grand staircase, the three-storied

Sir Arthur Evans, eighty-five years old, with Cretan exhibits at an exhibition of Greek antiquities in 1936. A model of the 'throne of Minos' can be seen in the centre, with pictures in the background showing reconstructions of the Palace of Knossos made by Piet de Jong.

buildings, the internal light-wells.

Evans' 'restoration' was so ruthless that it is hard to know what is genuine and what is not. For instance, of all those pillars, which for many of us are the hallmark of Knossos, not one is original: they are all creations of this century. Nevertheless the general layout of the palaces *is* original. What strikes us at once as we view Minoan palaces is their standard design, as standard as the dwelling-house of nineteenth-century London. There is a central court, surrounded by a number of chambers giving on to it. This occurs at Phaistos, at Mallia, at Zakro and at other less important sites. Some of the rooms were for habitation, others housed magazines for corn, wine and oil, and in great plenty, too. The notable thing about all the cities is that none of them is walled: they are all unfortified 'open cities'. This alone gives them a 'modern' look. The reason is that in their heyday the Minoans controlled the sea.

Here again the legend of the mission to Athens and the living tribute once exacted of that city comes in. It is clear from Plutarch's *Life of Theseus* that there were a number of contradictory stories regarding the relations of Crete with the mainland. The one thing that is certain is that, as Plutarch points out, Minos is universally, and in Plutarch's view unfairly, regarded as an aggressor, an oppressor of Athens and a revisher of Athenian youth, as a slave-raider in fact. His 'labyrinth' (the palace-complex at Knossos) was his prison. Peace is only made after the death of Minos, when Ariadne becomes queen in her own right, and Prince Theseus, returning with Daedalus and other exiles, makes a pact of perpetual friendship between Crete and Athens. This shows that after the fall of Knossos the see-saw tipped in the other direction, as it so often does, and that the victim became the victor, i.e. the Mycenean mainland dominated the island.

The prominence of Ariadne is of significance. There were, as Plutarch says 'many traditions about these things, and as many concerning Ariadne, all inconsistent with each other'. But that a female took a leading part in affairs is a pointer to a sophisticated society and that is just what Minoan society was. Whatever we may think of the putative quarters assigned to various characters (all imaginary) in Evans' Knossos, the 'throne-room'

*Opposite*
East of Knossos the land declines to a shallow ravine. The royal apartments lay on this side, terraced into the slope.

Knossos, the so-called throne room, discovered in April 1900. After the disaster of 1450 BC the room was probably a private shrine for the Priest-King. The throne is made of local gypsum. The decoration is Mycenaean in style: grandeur has replaced Minoan naturalism.

*Above*
The queen's megaron (hall), with a bathroom beyond.

*Right*
The painting dubbed 'La Parisienne', from the Camp-Stool fresco, which 'gives a marvellously vivacious picture of the courtiers who surrounded royalty . . . the first truly naturalistic style in ancient art and of the highest quality' (Reynold Higgins).

(probably a small chapel), the 'Queen's Megaron' and so on, there is no doubt that the Knossians of the grand epoch did live easy lives, the ladies clad with daring elegance, the men dressed and undressed with panache. Unfortunately silly names such as 'La Parisienne' were stuck on to figures reconstructed from fragments of fresco, suggesting a world like that of Offenbach and leaving Homer

quite out of account. What is important is that there *were* frescoes and that in their remains, however miniature, (before 'restoration') we do possess the earliest examples of European pictorial art. It is also beyond question that the palace folk of the latest epoch, if not earlier, enjoyed a good water-supply and commodious drains. To the Anglo-Saxon mind which equates civilization and plumbing this is of outstanding appeal.

The representations, both in fresco and in the round, of 'bull-leaping' are still a subject of conjecture. Were the lads (and lasses too, if we may believe the Cretan poet Kazantzakis) baiting the bull in play, or are the representations a stylization of a sacrificial function? Why is the bull in the well-known 'bull-dancer' gem sitting down? Spanish bull-fighters say that the 'vaulting' is impossible; but to anyone who has witnessed the space- and gravity-defying antics of the Russian State Circus these scenes of 'taking the bull by the horns' seem by no means fantastic. Dr Higgins reminds us that in the Landes district of France young men turn somersaults over charging cows.

Knossos remains a beacon. It tells us far more of truth than of fiction. To quote MacKendrick: 'Knossos was for about a century (1580–1480 BC) the centre of an international power, the first in European history.

'The wealth, enthusiasm, and imagination of Sir Arthur Evans reconstructed . . . not always, it is to be feared, with complete fidelity to the archaeological data, but the result is vivid, picturesque and colorful enough to satisfy the most jaded tourist; the bright frescoes; the famous downward-tapering painted cypress-wood columns; the huge storage jars, taller than a man, have been restored or left *in situ* to lend the Palace of Minos more human interest than any other prehistoric Greek site . . . One of the most rewarding sites to visit in the entire ancient world.'

The work of excavation is still continuing. In addition to his work on the palace Evans did much on the town of Knossos. In 1973 Dr Peter Warren, working for the British School in Athens, uncovered a new 'Royal Road' joining the old one and the public buildings. It was possibly a grandstand for watching processions on the south side of the Royal Road.

It may well be that Evans' first interest in Knossos will prove to have the most enduring value, namely his work in epigraphy. The discovery of 'Linear B' and the labours of Ventris and Chadwick have already been mentioned. Before leaving this dream-world of prehistory where the lights are so bright and the shadows so dark, just as they are in the Greek landscape to-day, it may be well to recall in brief the process which has given us our knowledge of this ancient art. These notes are based on Chapter I of *The Mycenaeans* by Lord William Taylour, by far the best and most lucid guide to this highly technical subject.

As early as 1900 Evans had observed clay tablets, incised, at Knossos, and had realized their importance. He deduced that since the tablets bore signs such as horses, chariots, weapons etc. they were day-to-day business records. Only in 1952 were the

The grand staircase in the east wing. It rises at least one storey above the central court and descends two storeys below it. One of Evans' most justifiable and evocative reconstructions.

many attempts at deciphering them crowned with success. In that year the talent of a young architect, Michael Ventris, who as a schoolboy had heard Evans lecture, allied with the knowledge of a Cambridge philologist, John Chadwick, succeeded in deciphering Linear B, as Evans had named the script. As Lord William points out: 'To understand this colossal achievement one must appreciate that Ventris was attempting a far more difficult task than the problem that faced Champollion in solving the riddle of Egyptian hieroglyphics or Grotefend and Rawlinson in the decipherment of cuneiform. These early pioneers had bilingual or trilingual texts to help them and at least they knew the linguistic groups to which the language belonged. Ancient Egyptian, though much modified, lived on in the Coptic tongue; Assyrian and Babylonian were related, it became clear, to ancient Hebrew and Semitic languages in general. But Ventris was faced with one script alone and without a clue as to what language it might stand for'.

Many had preceded Ventris in the apparently hopeless quest. Evans himself was a pioneer. He was able to shew the different stages in the script's development – hieroglyphic signs of the first half of the second millenium, then a cursive and simplified version of these signs, which Sir Arthur termed Linear A. Finally he identified a more advanced script closely related to Linear A, which he called Linear B. Linear A overlapped the hieroglyphs, and seems to have gone out in the early part of the fifteenth century. Linear B, which is almost wholly on tablets, came in about 1400 BC. It is the only form of the script to be known on the Greek mainland.

Evans established certain basic points: that the tablets were list of accounts; that a numerical system was clearly recognizable, that some of the signs were pictures of the objects indicated, and that the others were probably syllabic.

As usual 'scholars' started guessing. Scholars are not immune from the law of Humpty-Dumpty, that facts must be the slaves of theory: 'When *I* use a word, it means just what I choose it to mean, neither more nor less.' But an American scholar, Dr Alice E. Kober, followed the facts. She was able to shew that Linear B was an inflected language: she found in it such variants as in English might be 'wo-man', wo-man's; wo-men'. These are known in linguistic circles as 'Kober's triplets'. Professor

Emmett L. Bennett Jr. was able to elucidate the system of weights and measures used in the script, and to classify the whole of the Linear B signary into two classes, ideographic and syllabic. He reduced the number of syllabic signs to ninety.

This preliminary work by the two American scholars was invaluable to Ventris, who now applied to the problem a knowledge of cryptography. In theory, any code (but not every bi-numerical cipher) can be 'cracked' by observing recurring features and underlying patterns. Ventris applied the methods used by Cambridge scholars in two wars on enemy codes to Linear B. He was thus able to construct a 'grid' consisting of 15 rows of consonants and 5 columns of vowels. But what language did these signs expound? Ventris thought they were Etruscan, a tongue we still cannot read. Only as 'a frivolous digression' (his own words) did he experiment with Greek. To his amazement, it worked: many of the tablets at last made sense. Greek it was, archaic, outmoded Greek, but still Greek. Naturally his claim was disputed. But just as he was reaching his solution Blegen was studying a tablet in Athens, one of 400 discovered during the 1952 season at Pylos. He tried Ventris' syllabary on it, and found that it had a tale to tell. It was clearly an inventory relating to tripods (a form of table dearly loved by Greeks, if only because on their uneven ground a tripod will always stand firm, where a four-legged table – *trapeza* – will wobble, as it does in every Greek taverna to-day.)

This is the outline of one of the great treasure-hunts of history. The prize belongs to us all.

In or about 1450 BC yet another catastrophe struck Crete, which afflicted all the major sites in the island. No one knows what caused it. Since Crete is in a notoriously seismic region, it may well have been the earthquakes associated with the explosion of the island of Thera (Santorin), itself a vast volcano, which then occurred. This thanks to American investigation of the adjacent seabed, is known to have deposited showers of lava, and it must also have generated a colossal tidal wave, which would have struck mainland Greece about the region of Troezen. This gave rise to the legend of the 'Bull from the Sea', i.e. something monstrous from the direction of Crete, the same bull which destroyed Hippolytus, as vividly described in the play of that name by Euripides (see Chapter VIII).

After the disaster there was a partial recovery, most speedily at Knossos. Some other sites were reoccupied, such as Gournia, Mallia, Palaiokastro, Tyllisos and Zakro. Many of the country villas were left desolate. The time was out of joint, and in accordance with Malthus' first law of population men now, in a time of insecurity, took to the hilltops.

By the eighth century BC Crete is a flourishing Dorian island, aswim in the main stream of Hellenism. It is no longer unique. Only once more will it be damned to everlasting fame, when St Paul, quoting a Greek poet, tells Titus that the Cretans are nothing but a herd of lying gluttons. Night had followed day as night inevitably does: but what a glorious day it had been, what a dayspring it had shed upon mankind.

The famous charioteer, dedicated by Polyzelus of Gela, in Sicily. Original bronze by the sculptor Sotades of Thespiae in Delphi. Fourth century BC, now in the Delphi Museum.

# CHAPTER VII
# The Heart of Hellas

'The eagles build, and the bronze charioteer drives undismayed towards infinity.' Thus did E. M. Forster sum up Delphi.

Knossos had been the capital of a great empire, Mycenae the mistress of a grand confederation. Crete had flourished behind the wooden walls of her sea-power, *thalassokratía* as the Greeks sonorously styled it, Mycenae by steel and by gold. One centre, and one only, was Hellas to have which would owe its immense sway to the spirit alone.

The site of Delphi is one of the most impressive in the whole world. It possesses the primordial elements of grandeur: twin peaks of tawny-grey rock which stand sentinel at the foot of Mount Parnassus; a perennial spring, a valley cleft from out great rocks; an olive-grove by a river – the largest olive-grove in Greece; and to close the vista, two thousand feet below, the silver-blue sea of Hellas. The site for this most august of all oracles was chosen, men said, by Zeus himself. He despatched two eagles, one from the eastward heaven and one from the west, and where they met, there was the shrine ordained to stand, at Delphi, the navel of the world.

As a shrine and oracle of Apollo Delphi was to be supreme not only in Greece but in countries far beyond her bounds. Originally, that is certainly as early as the second millenium BC, it was Ge, the Earth-Mother, who presided here. That was natural; and did not Poseidon, the Shaker of Earth, aid and abet her, with seismic fury? Did not that crystal spring of never-failing abundance bring light and life to men from the dark womb of Earth itself? At first the place was named Pytho, and was so called by Homer. The oracle was presided over by the priestess Pythia, near the cave of the serpent Python, son of Mother Earth. Primitive Pytho was in the territory of Krisa, in the plain below, and to Krisa was brought from Crete the cult of Apollo Delphinios, or 'of the Dolphin', a typically Greek synthesis.

Apollo was the most gracious and light-bearing of the gods, the author and giver of all good things. When the Romans took over the Greek pantheon to re-stock their own meagre and dreary heaven, they assimilated a Greek deity to each of their twelve gods – all except Apollo. He was too far above any Roman imagining, and so he alone retains his Greek name, Apollo in Latin no less than in Greek. Of all marine creatures the dolphin, down to our own day, has always been regarded as the friend of man. Herodotus tells us how a dolphin saved the harpist Arion from death, and Pliny has the story of a dolphin who used to carry a little boy on his back across the Bay of Naples to school at Puteoli every morning and then take him back in the evening. Dolphins were popular with Cretan wall-artists. It was natural therefore that when Apollo came to Pytho he should be associated with the dolphin (Greek *delphis*) and that the shrine should henceforth be called Delphi. The fact that *delphys* means a womb in Greek may have assisted the transition.

Apollo slew the Python, and so the shrine of Delphi was now and always known as the oracle of *Pythian Apollo*. Later on, business became so brisk that the god Dionysus was associated with him, and then Athena, the Temple Guardian (*Pronaia*) or Providence (*Pronoia*). During the three winter months, when Apollo was away in the far north, Dionysus stood in for him at Delphi.

The human direction of Delphi was confided (after the Doric invasion, c. 1100 BC) to an association called the Amphictionic League, meaning the league of these who 'dwell around' a locality. The association was composed of twelve tribes, each of which contained various city-states great and small, and all of which, be they Athens or Sparta, or more humble dwellers in Thessaly, Boeotia or Phokis, had equal status within the league. 'This rudimentary United Nations', as the Blue Guide aptly calls it, had to withstand attempts by greedy neighbours of Delphi to become masters of so lucrative a shrine. Krisa was the first agressor, and thus occurred the *First* Sacred War (c. 595–586 BC) after which the plain of Krisa was sequestrated, and no one was allowed to till it or seek pasture in it. Delphi became autonomous under the League, and entered on its first great period of affluence. Pious donations came from far and wide, including offerings from king Croesus of Lydia, of no avail in his case. Amasis of Egypt, the first man to whom the epithet

The Castalian spring, east of the sanctuary. The basin is cut from the rock and there are votive niches where pilgrims took a ritual bath before entering the precinct of Apollo.

'philhellene' was applied (by Herodotus) earned his title by his benefactions to Delphi. If Olympia was the national focus of Hellas, Delphi was its international centre.

In 548 BC the temple was destroyed by fire, and the noble Athenian exiles, the Alkmaeonidae, having obtained the contract for rebuilding it, increased not only the prestige of the shrine but of themselves, by constructing the new temple in marble imported, at vast expense in transport charges, from the island of Paros, instead of using the local stone.

In 480, despite the oracle's pro-Persian leanings, Xerxes sent a troop to loot Delphi. It had got as far as the temple of Athena Pronoia when amid a thunderstorm down came great lumps of rock which crushed many of the marauders to death.

Although universally famous, the oracle was not always trusted. It was becoming corrupted by the power which 'always tends to corrupt'. But its international repute stood it in good stead when it became the catalyst of mere individual woes and problems. During the peak period of Greek colonization, that is from the eighth to the sixth centuries BC, it has been computed that some 159 colonies were founded, in regions as far apart as the Black Sea and Spain. In many cases the colonists had been advised by Delphi where to plant their settlements, and what gods they should worship. Byzantium and Cyrene are among the best known. Once established it continued to be the custom for settlements, as well as states and persons, to seek the oracle's advice. Should we make war? Should we embark on a voyage, lend money, or marry? Parke and Wormell in *The Delphic Oracle*, have collected 600 such questions and answers.

Thus the shrine continued to be extremely opulent. Either you brought an offering to win the god's favour, or to thank him for having shown it to you, or both. Just how the oracle operated we do now know. Only male enquirers were admitted, and a preliminary purification at the spring and a sacrifice, generally of a goat, were obligatory. The postulants assembled outside the *adyton*, or innermost

shrine, and there awaited their turn, unless they had been granted special precedence, *promanteia*, as it was called. An inscription of 322 on the base of the base of the Naxian monument records that they were among those who possessed it. In antiquity the belief was well founded that the priestess sat on a tripod over a crevice, from which issued stupifying fumes, or that the cyanide in the laurel which she chewed threw her into a trance. To-day there is no crevice in the enclosure, nor are there any fumes. It is just possible that in so earthquake-prone an area there may once have been both. Whatever the circumstances, in historic times the priestess was an elderly virgin, and when the question was put to her, she uttered the answer in ambiguous ejaculations, which were then reduced to hexameters, generally as ambiguous, by the attendant priest. In all ages elderly virgins have not seldom been psychologically impressionable; and a mediumistic form of possession is the most rational explanation of the phenomena of oracular utterance in an era which drew no definite distinction between the natural and supernatural. Virgil, who may be taken as 'the master of them that know', makes his Sibyl (*Aeneid VI, 77 seq*) contend against a possessing god, as a horse tries to throw its rider, but is forced to give in to him. This was no doubt how an elderly female hierophant, the only representative of her sex in all-male company, would react to the mystic ambiance.

Antiquity, setting, topography – for it really could claim to be the world's navel – all contributed to the primacy of Delphi. Just how much of its authority came from its political alignment, it is hard to say. It discouraged opposition to Persia, although this did not deter Xerxes from trying to loot it, nor the Athenians from dedicating Persian spoils there – after they had beaten the Persians. It was pro-Spartan in the Peloponnesian War; it backed Philip of Macedon. It had favoured Croesus the great king of Lydia, and yet in a famous piece of ambiguity foretold that by crossing the river Halys, the boundary between his kingdom and the realm of Persia, he would destroy a great empire. He did: it was his own.

Against this ambiguous political attitude, which has had more than one parallel in later ages, it must be stressed that in matters of personal morality Delphi was strict. When the oracle was asked if there were any man wiser than Sokrates, it answered unequivocally 'No'. On the walls of the temple were inscribed the proto-Puritan mottoes 'Know thyself' and 'Nothing in excess'. Delphi's most famous citizen is one of its latest, namely Plutarch, who lived in the latter part of the first century AD and the early years of the second. He was proud of being a son of Chaeronea, in Boeotia, proud of his honorary Athenian citizenship; but it was as a moralist that he saw himself, and he took his duties as a priest of Delphi very seriously. He was a true servant of Apollo.

In 448 BC there occurred the *Second* Sacred War, when the Spartans wrested Delphi from the Phokians, who had occupied it, and handed it over to the Delphians. As soon as they withdrew the Athenians seized it, and handed it back to the

*Above*
Delphi, looking back to the
road from Athens, across the
ruins of Apollo's temple.

*Left*
A view of Delos from Mount
Kynthos. The birthplace of
Apollo and his sister Artemis,
Delos was a sacred island
to the Greeks and is
mentioned in the *Odyssey*.

Phokians. The Delphians soon recovered it, and
their possession was confirmed by the Peace of Nikias
in 421 BC, which proclaimed a fifty year truce
between Athens and Sparta. (The truce lasted for
six years only.)

In retrospect, there is something childish about
these Nuts-in-May manoeuverings, as there is in so
much that is Greek. In 373 the temple was again
destroyed, by an earthquake. Once again in 356 the
Phokians, indignant at having been fined by the
Amphictionic League for cultivating a part of the
forbidden Krisaean Plain, seized Delphi with all its
accumulated treasure. This precipitated the *Third*
Sacred War, during which Phokis became for a
season one of the leading powers of Greece. In 346,
when Philip of Macedon was already casting his
shadow over Hellas, the League won back the
custody of Delphi. Philip replaced Phokis in the
League and became president of the Pythian Games.
Yet a *Fourth* Sacred War broke out in 119. It
was the Amphissians who had this time encroached
upon the sacrosanct Plain. The Amphictians
appealed to Philip, who invaded Greece. He won
the battle of Chaeronea, and destroyed the guilty
city of Amphissa, in neighbouring Lokris. He also
destroyed Greek independence.

As may be inferred from the foregoing brief
resumé of the stormy and violent vicissitudes of a
city which was dedicated to peace, Delphi had now
passed its zenith. Barbarian Gauls invaded it in 279,
only to be repulsed, like the Persians, by supernatural intervention. In 189 the Aetolians, last Greek
guardians of Delphi, were ousted by the Romans.

Sulla plundered the precinct in 86. An oracle
meant little to the hard-headed and hard-hearted
Romans. Nero stole more than 500 bronze statues
(think of it, 500 *bronzes*!) in a fit of rage at the oracle's
condemnation of him for having murdered his
mother, the empress Agrippina. But a little later,
Pliny counted 3,000 statues: they must have been as
thick on the ground as a magnified asparagus-bed;
an average of about one to every five square yards.
Domitian had favoured Delphi, and so did the last
of the philhellenes, the emperor Hadrian, who introduced into the liturgy the veneration of his boy
favourite Antinoüs, of whom the statue in the Delphi
museum is one of the most poignant we possess.
Constantine filched the Plataean tripod and much
else to adorn his new Rome, Constantinople. Julian
the Apostate thought of reviving the oracle, but it
was the once sacred voice itself which informed him
that its times had gone by, and that the rest was
silence. This was formally confirmed in AD 385 by the
Christian emperor Theodosius. It had been vocal
for two thousand years.

In its heyday Delphi, in accordance with the
Greek canon of excellence which included every
faculty of man, had a theatre, for dramatic repre-

sensations, and a stadium for athletic competitions.

The games were at first celebrated at eight-yearly intervals. From 582, when Delphi was at the height of its influence, they were reorganized and held every four years. Only under the Roman decline did they revert to the eight-year cycle.

For centuries Delphi was forgotten and neglected. In 1436 Cyriacus of Ancona was copying inscriptions here. The site was again forgotten, until in 1676 Wheler and Spon rediscovered it. Flaubert records that in 1851 he found Byron's name, inscribed on a now vanished column, with that of his friend Hobhouse. So impressed was Byron by the site that he inserted several verses about it in the context of a description of the young ladies of Seville (*Childe Harold*, I, lx). It is mid-December, 1809.

> Oh, thou Parnassos! whom I now survey,
> Now in the phrensy of a dreamer's eye,
> Not in the fabled landscape of a lay,
> But soaring snow-clad through thy native sky,
> In the wild pomp of mountain majesty!
> What marvel if I thus essay to sing?
> The humblest of thy pilgrims passing by
> Would gladly woo thine echoes with his string,
> Though from thy heights no more one Muse will
>      wave her wing.

Byron was twenty-two when he wrote that. No one had written like it before; and although many since then think that they have, the Greeks still know that they have not. Greeks have been, and still often are wrong; but they have always been right about Byron.

In 1838 the French architect Laurent examined the site. In 1840 it was visited by Gottfried Müller, who caught a fever there and died, and by Ernst Curtius, who in 1852 stimulated the plans for the excavation of Olympia. After preliminary examination in 1860–61 by French scholars, the French School at Athens, under Théophile Homolle began systematic excavation in 1892, having 'won the excavation rights from the Americans by removing their import duty on Greek currants' (MacKendrick). A whole village had to be removed and rehoused, not without opposition and bloodshed. The French government paid the entire cost, about £30,000 in those days, and the villagers have grown rich on French enterprise ever since. 'An incomplete German description of the buildings and monuments lists 235 items, and the museum inventory, which does not list all the finds, catalogues over 7,000 objects, some of them, like the bronze charioteer, world famous. Inscriptions were so numerous that the excavations director sometimes found himself obliged to transcribe 100 a day.' (*ibid*)

It is a hard task to comprehend so sprawling a sanctuary, which is at the same time the most cluttered and complicated in all Greece. Despite the enormous number of 'finds' mentioned above, not one of the offerings mentioned by Pausanias has survived. How we should have delighted to see, for instance, the Athenian gift of a bronze palm-tree, with golden dates, surmounted by a golden statue of Athena; and what a shock it would give to those who

*Above*
The partially reconstructed *Tholos* (rotunda). It is not known to whom the building was dedicated.

*Left*
The stadium at Delphi, looking west. There was room for 7,000 spectators.

like to harp on the 'restraint' of Athenian taste, in which they see a justification for their own repressions.

The French, with commendable skill and sense of proportion, have made no attempt to 're-construct' Delphi as Evans did Knossos. All they have done is to clear the site, by moving thousands of tons of soil, excavate the theatre and the stadium, re-erect a few buildings such as the Athenian Treasury, and put up a few columns in the Marmaria and the temple

*Right*
Delos. The 'House of
Hermes', built towards the
end of the third century BC,
is the oldest three-storey
house known to us.

*Below*
Rhodes..The ruins of
Athena's temple at Lindos,
on a perpendicular cliff 400
feet above the sea. Fourth
century BC.

*Below, right*
Of the great temple of
Artemis at Ephesus, one of
the seven wonders of the
ancient world, nothing
remains but a few beautiful
marbles in the world's
great museums. This
fragment of a carved column
shows Alkestis with the god
Hermes, who carries the
*kerykeion* or herald's staff.
Mid-fourth century BC, now
in the British Museum.

of Apollo. All else must be learned from a guide, human or written, and complemented by the exhibits in the museum, which is a model of its kind.

It is best to approach the site as Plutarch and Pausanias did, from the east. We come first to the Marmaria, a modern name for the precinct below the modern road, and the spring Castalia which only too ominously reflects the ignoble abuse to which it has been subjected–that of a marble-quarry. Nevertheless the French have cleared a large part of the precinct. We first come upon the oldest part of the sanctuary, dedicated to Athena of Health, and of the Girdle (symbol of chastity?), where in 1922 a Mycenaean settlement came to light. Then we come to the remnants of the old temple of Athene Pronoia, of the early fifth century BC on the site of a still older shrine of the seventh. This temple was damaged by the rock-fall which routed the Persians, and was wrecked by the earthquake of 373. Fifteen columns had been brought to light when in 1905 another landslide demolished all but three of them.

The centre of the precinct is occupied by three buildings: a Doric treasury of marble on a limestone foundation, and a Treasury of Massalia, or Marseilles, a remarkably fine structure of Parian marble, which must have given its French excavators proud satisfaction. The third building is the *Tholos*, or rotunda. To whom it was dedicated, and with what intent we do not know; but of its twenty slender Doric columns three, with their entablature, were re-erected in 1938, to grace one of the most famous and beautiful travel-posters of our day. After the new temple of Athena, we come to the gymnasium, as rebuilt by the Romans. There is nothing Spartan, or even Olympic-like about it. It has a *xystos*, or covered practise-colonnade for use in bad weather, and a parallel open-air track. Below there is a *palaistra* or wrestling-ground, complete with cold and hot showers and baths. No better evidence could we have of what Delphi had become in Roman hands – a personal enquiry bureau, with recreation facilities attached. Against this background, Plutarch's devotion stands out all the more brightly.

Crossing the road, we come to the famous Castalian spring, with its seven antique fountain-houses. It was the Romans, not the Greeks, who attributed poetic power to it: Ovid sings,

*Vilia miretur vulgus: mihi flavus Apollo*
*Pocula Castalia plena ministret aqua*
(Let the crowd gape at trash. Fair-haired Apollo!
Give me Castalian drafts galore to swallow!)

The temple of Apollo at Didyma, twenty miles south of Miletus in Asia Minor. It was so large (259 by 150 feet) that the roofing of the main hall was never completed. The columns, 120 of them, were 65 feet high. The temple was in the care of an hereditary priesthood, who waxed fat on the rich offerings it attracted. Building was begun in 313 BC and went on until AD 41.

It is indeed something 'as holy and enchanted' as Coleridge's famous chasm, that echoing cascade with the great Shining Rocks, as they were called, soaring above it.

Moving east, purified in mind as the ancient postulants were in body, we enter the *temenos*, meaning the 'separated area' of the god, from the Greek *temnein*, to cut. Owing to the sloping nature of the ground, the whole area is but 200 yards by 140. Overcrowding was inevitable, given the Greek passion for going one better than your neighbour, so that competitive ostentation has guided the nature and position of many of the memorials. The Sacred Way is between 12 and 16 feet wide, and the French have considerably restored the steps. Among those who dedicated memorials here were an Aeginetan who had made a big profit from tunny-fishing; the Arcadians, to score off their rivals the Spartans whose monument is opposite; the Spartans to laud the admiral who had trounced the Athenians; the men of Argos in honour of the Messenians, hereditary foes of the Spartans. Then we have one raised by the citizens of Taranto, the chief Greek city of southern Italy. The whole ascent has the aspect of a row of pavilions at an international exhibition.

We now take a hairpin bend in the Way, and the great series of Treasuries is around us. Those of the Sicyonians, Corinth's western neighbours, and that of the Siphnians, we have already passed. Standing on the left of the curve itself, is the beautifully reconstructed Treasury of the Athenians originally built from the spoils of Marathon. More than 150 inscriptions adorn the walls, including two humns to Apollo, with the original musical notation which no one understands. Immediately opposite we are not surprised to find the Treasury of the Syracusans, built to commemorate their rout of the Athenians in 413. Knidos and Cyrene had treasuries too. Altogether there were no less than twenty-three; here, as at Olympia, memorial, consulate and safe-deposit in one.

After passing the senate-house or *bouleuterion*, a plain rectangular building, we ascend past the inevitable assembly of tripods to the altar and temple of Apollo. In front of its great polygonal wall, which is a masterpiece of masonry in itself, its form being calculated to resist earthquake shocks, once stood the portico in which the Athenians hung up the cables with which Xerxes had secured his bridge of boats across the Hellespont in 480 BC. (Two thousand three hundred and thirteen years later, the Hellespont is once again spanned by cables, of electric power-lines and, for the first time since Xerxes, by bridge-cables, those of the new suspension-bridge between Europe and Asia). The wall is covered with inscriptions, many of which record the liberation of slaves, whose dedication to Apollo secured their freedom.

The temple itself, the third to stand on the site, is disappointing, with little more than its ground-

The Athenian treasury at Delphi, built from the spoils of the battle of Marathon. Inscriptions on the walls include two hymns to Apollo with the original musical notation.

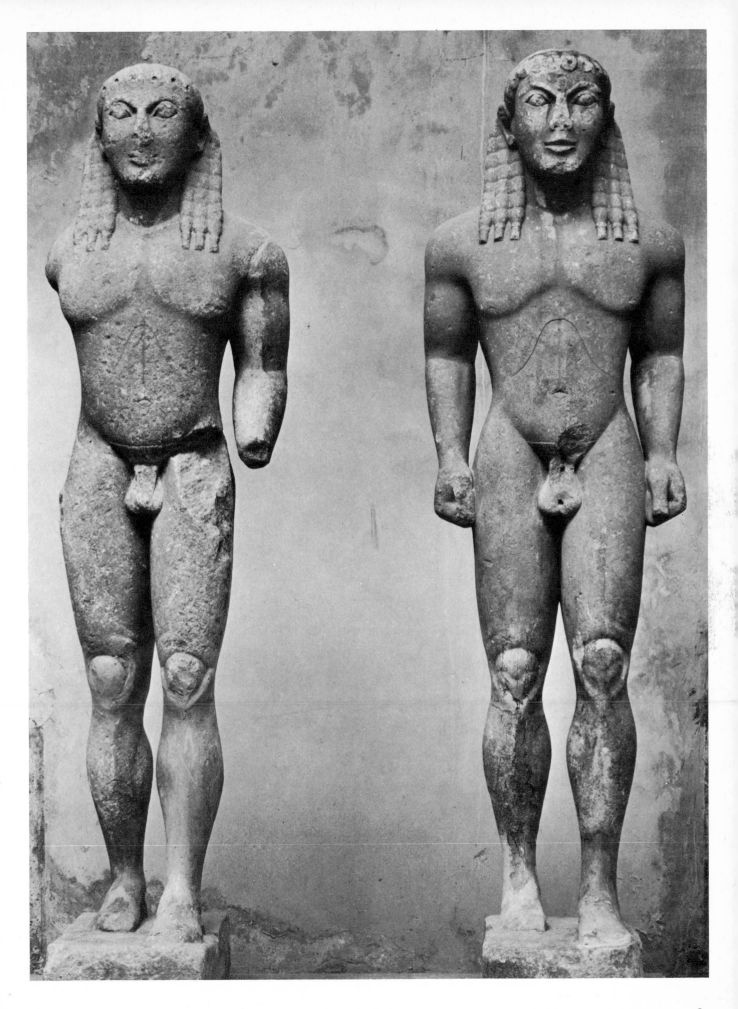

*Below*
In the Stoa of Attalus, rebuilt to the original design of the first century BC by the American School to house the antiquities excavated in the Agora. The perfect proportions and classical style make it a haven of restful coolness as well as a beautiful museum.

*Bottom*
Ephesus, showing the Arcadian Way and the great theatre, the scene of the silversmiths' riot described in the Acts of the Apostles.

*Right*
The famous Naxian lions of Delos, and general view of the precinct of Apollo.

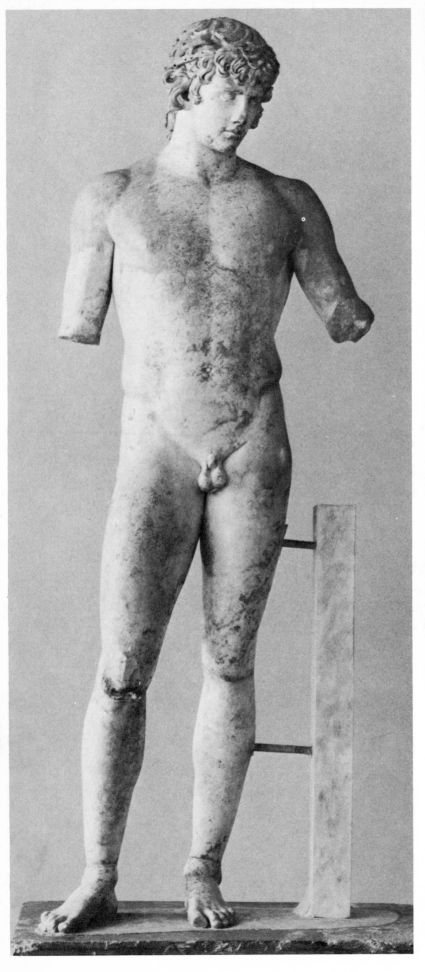

plan surviving, though here again the tactful re-erection of six columns is a help to comprehension. As usual, the Middle-Agers, in their lust for metal, wrenched the stones apart to get at the dowels, thus completing a ruin which time and earthquakes had begun. That the *adyton* was an underground chamber is about all we know of the functioning of this celebrated shrine. Not a fragment of the pediments described by Pausanias has survived.

Above the temple is the theatre, one of the best preserved in Greece. The view from the auditorium is incomparable: how could the most talented cast have competed against it? Finally we come to the stadium, 2,116 feet above the level of the sea. Herodes Atticus once again provided the seats, enough for 7,000 spectators. On the outside of the

*Opposite*
Antinoüs, the Bithynian favourite of the philhellene emperor Hadrian (AD 117–138). More than 500 busts and statues of Antinoüs survive but this, one of the best, may well have been done from life. Antinoüs was drowned in the Nile in AD 130, while travelling with Hadrian. The emperor deified him after his death. Delphi Museum.

The theatre, overlooking the temple of Apollo. The original structure was of the fourth century BC, and this was rebuilt in the second by Eumenes I, King of Pergamum. It seated 5,000 people.

southern wall of the stadium, at the eastern end, is an inscription which imposes a fine of five drachmas on anyone who takes new wine out of (not into) the precinct. This has puzzled many. The reason is that the whole precinct was sacred to Apollo, and all that therein was; and so any secularization of its gifts would be sacrilege. What more charming, more Greek way could there be of reminding the pilgrim of his status and the importance of his goal?

The museum houses many treasures, among them sculptures from the Sicyonian and Siphnian Treasuries, the athlete Agias and the statues of Kleobis and Biton mentioned by Herodotus. These were two heroes who, when the oxen which were to draw their mother's car to a festival at Argos did not arrive, drew her to Argos themselves. She was a priestess of Argos, and her sons were rewarded by Hera at her request with the greatest possible blessing – that is death. The Greek preference for death over life is one of their most paradoxical qualities. These two statues are the largest of Parian marble yet found on the Greek mainland.

Above all there is the charioteer. This was found in 1896, together with the inscription of Polyzalos of Sicily who dedicated it probably to celebrate victory in a chariot race at the Pythian games in 474. Pausanias never saw it, because it had been thrown down and buried by the earthquake of 373 BC. Only after the war of 1939–45 was it expertly photographed and studied, in Athens whither it had been consigned for safety. It is cast by the process known as *cire perdue*, which is of great antiquity. The

The Odeum of Herodes Atticus, a present from a wealthy philhellene Roman to the people of Athens in AD 160 to commemorate his dead wife. It is still used as a theatre.

sculptor prepares a core of gypsum, in the form he wishes his finished work to assume. This is covered with wax and then encased in a shell of the same material, gypsum, leaving an interval between it and the core. The molten bronze is now poured into the space between shell and core, and the wax is melted and 'lost' through vents left for the purpose. When the metal cooled, the gypsum core was extracted, the shell discarded, and the now hollow bronze stood free. The lips, as here, might be of copper, soldered on, the paste eyes, with iris in brown (magnesium) and pupils in black (onyx) inserted. The victor's fillet hides the join of the two pieces in which the head was cast, thus enabling the eyes to be placed from the inside. The hair was engraved, the whole sculpture polished. MacKendrick compares this masterpiece to 'an ode of Pindar, with which it is contemporary, and like it, it is hieratic, forceful, controlled, finished, intellectualized, a splendid example of the severe style'.

It is also a splendid example of metallurgy: the whole work was cast in only seven parts, head, torso, lower half and the four limbs, the girdle being added on completion.

Delphi at sunrise, when the already incandescent plain below casts its reflection westwards to the still shadowed chasm and precinct above; Delphi at the rise of the full moon, when the great copper disc sheds its slow radiance on the silvery peaks above the velvet depths; Delphi in its now rare silences, when the nightingales oust the transistors, or in its international, traditional bustle and chatter, Delphi is still the heart of Hellas. When you hear it beat, it makes your own heart beat more bravely.

The Akropolis in the glow
of the setting sun. The
marble of the most
celebrated site in the world
shows gold against the
darkening sky, while in the
city below an audience
gathers for a performance in
the Odeum.

# CHAPTER VIII
# Isles of Greece

When Byron went to Greece in 1810 he visited more places on the mainland of Hellas than any Englishman had ever visited before. Even to-day, with travel cushioned and accelerated by modern devices, it would be a hardy tourist who would attempt to follow in his footsteps. Yet it was this same Byron who in one of the best-known lyrics in the language apostrophized 'The isles of Greece, the isles of Greece!'

It would be impossible even to catalogue all the islands which spangle the Greek seas. In the Aegean, from classical times, two main groups have been recognized, the Cyclades (circling, i.e. around Delos) and the Sporades (scattered). The Cyclades number over thirty in all, though Strabo reckoned only twelve or fifteen important enough to qualify. The Sporades were originally the islands off the west coast of Asia Minor, the majority of which are known as the Dodecanese, or Twelve Islands, with the addition of Chios, Samos, Lesbos and the Western Sporades, of which Skiathos and Skopelos are the best known. In a book of limited scope it will be possible to mention only some of this galaxy.

Being himself a poet, Byron naturally saluted first his sister-poet, 'burning Sappho', who adorned the island of Lesbos or Mytilene in the seventh and sixth centuries BC; the home also of Terpander, father of Greek music, Arion the harpist, who was rescued by the dolphin, and Alcaeus, the lyric poet of the seventh century. No other island was such a nest of singing-birds. Prehistoric remains indicate habitation from about 3300 BC. According to Homer, Lesbos sided with Troy and was invaded both by Achilles and by Odysseus. Its fine harbour favoured maritime enterprise, which embraced lands as far distant as Egypt. In 527 Lesbos fell under the Persian yoke; but she regained her freedom in 479 and joined the Athenian League. In 428, soon after the beginning of the Peloponnesian War, Mytilene tried to break away from the League. The Athenians decreed a ruthless punishment, of which they at once repented, and a second galley arrived just in time to rescue those condemned to death by the despatches carried in the first.

Mithridates occupied the island from 88 to 79 BC, and Julius Caesar won his spurs during the subsequent Roman reoccupation. We can still see not only impressive Genoese, Turkish and Byzantine relics, but also the Greek theatre, which served Pompey as a model for his theatre in Rome – the first stone theatre to be constructed there.

The only island which Byron mentions by name in that immortal stanza is Delos, where 'Phoebus' (Apollo) 'sprung'. As usual, Byron is our best guide; for of all the islands it is Delos that calls us back most surely again and again. Its fascination is as hard to explain as it is to escape from. It is because it is now inhabited by phantoms only? Or that they are the phantoms of so many diverse gods and men? Or simply that it is, physically speaking, so unattractive; that here man far from being vile has nothing to fear from the scenery? The reason may lie in the very multiplicity of its attractions.

Most sites, be they on the mainland or among the islands, are famous for one thing; a shrine, as at Olympia, a building or complex of buildings as at Knossos or Rhodes, or an oracle as at Dodona or Delphi; but Delos has a triple charm. It was the birthplace of Apollo, and that made it the religious and political centre of the Aegean. It later became a great international market-place; and it contains the vestiges of a town of the Hellenistic age which is as evocative of those who dwelt in it as Herculaneum or Pompeii.

As a shrine of Apollo, as a panhellenic centre Delos was second only to Delphi. Nowhere in Greek poetry do we find a more lyrical invocation of the Greek joy in living than in the Homeric hymn to Apollo. To quote Guy Pentreath in his *Hellenic Traveller*. 'Delos begins with its god. The island was Apollo's birthplace. Zeus himself moored this hitherto roving island with adamantine chains, says tradition, that it might be a secure resting-place for Leto for the birth of Apollo and Artemis.' Delos became the meeting-place of Greeks from the twelve Ionian cities of Asia Minor and from the Greek mainland, though whether Apollo came from Asia Minor or from the lands of the Hyperboreans is still in dispute.

The Homeric hymn describes the festival on Delos:

'Many temples and woody groves and all the heights and jutting capes of lofty hills are dear to

The Erechtheium on the Akropolis, in soft morning light. The temple commemorated a site sacred to the Athenians; here stood the house of Erechtheus, the semi-divine, legendary king of Athens who was reared by the goddess Athena. The temple was completed in 407 BC.

you, and rivers that flow to the sea. But in Delos, O Apollo, does your heart most rejoice. There in your honour the long-robed Ionians gather together with their children and their noble wives. They delight you and celebrate you with boxing and dancing and song whenever they hold festival. A man would say they were immortal and free for ever from old age who should visit them when the Ionians are met together; for he would behold the grace of them all, and rejoice his heart seeing the men and the fair-girt women, and their swift ships and all their gear.'

Delos was originally called Ortygia, 'quail island'. That it was inhabited at the end of the third millenium BC is proved by the remains of a pre-historic settlement at the summit of its only hill, Mount Kynthos (whence the name Cynthia for Artemis.) From a very early date it was a religious centre. It is small, three miles long by less than one broad, it is barren, it has no spring and only this one hill, a mere 370 feet high. Perhaps it was chosen for its very insignificance, its uncovetableness in an age hungry for land and tilth.

By the seventh century BC, under the protection of

Naxos, Delos was the acknowledged centre of the Cyclades. The Athenians always maintained that the Greeks of Ionia were originally Athenians – refugees from the Dorian invaders, and so claimed that they, men of Athens, should protect their kin. Besides, Delos, tiny Delos, had such prestige throughout the region that to be its 'protector' would bring renown out of all proportion to the labour and expense involved. It was not only the eighth-century hymn which had lauded the island: Pindar, always in the vogue, hailed it: 'O daughter of the sea, thou unmoved wonder of the wide earth, whom mortals call Delos, but known to the blessed dwellers on Olympus as the far-seen star of the deep dark earth.'

The Athenians were great respecters of antiquity. For them it was their own Athena who had led Leto thither, letting her pause in Attica, as Patrick Anderson reminds us in his *The Smile of Apollo*, to shed her girdle near the modern bathing-beach of Vouliagmeni. Odysseus himself had seen Leto's palm tree, and was able to compare Nausikaä, daughter of king Alkinous, to it for her stately beauty. Theseus of Athens stopped in Delos on his way back after killing the Minotaur, and performed a ritual dance there with his rescued companions.

Like so many others, the Athenians sent religious embassies every year to Delos, the most famous of which delayed the death of Sokrates, since no execution might take place during the absence of the sacred vessels from Athens, and thus gave us his final discourse on the immortality of the soul which we know as the *Phaidon*.

The dealings of Athens with Delos were singularly tortuous, even for one of the crookedest democracies the world has ever seen. To start with under the cloak of piety the Athenians decreed that the island must be 'purified' and that no one might be born or die there. This meant that only citizens chosen by Athens might live there. When death approached, the moribund was conveyed to the island of Rheneia, which Polycrates of Samos had attached to Delos by chains and dedicated to Apollo. The first such 'purification' was ordained by Peisistratos, the Athenian ruler in 543. A second took place at the Athenians' behest in 426. 'No good,' as Pentreath

writes, 'assuring the sick man that this was just a change of air: he knew that soon after this first crossing the grimmer ferryman, Charon, would take him on another.'

Meanwhile Athens had brought off another *coup* at the expense not only of Delos but of many others besides. So firmly was the sanctity of the island established that in 490, during the Persian invasion Datis, the Persian admiral, had spared Delos. It therefore seemed to be a good centre for the *Delian* (i.e. Athenian) Confederacy and there its treasury was kept. But in 454, at the alleged suggestion of Samos, the treasury was transferred on 'security' grounds to Athens, where the 'surplus' came in very useful for embellishing the Akropolis with the monuments we still behold there. Athens restored the Delian Festival, which had lapsed in the course of years, and instituted the Delian Games.

In 422 the Athenians overreached themselves. They ordered the banishment of the few remaining island-born Delians – a measure they were obliged to revoke on the insistence of the Delphic oracle.

Delos, with the neighbouring island of Rheneia in the background. The building in the foreground – the House of Cleopatra – dates from the second century BC.

Looking across the old
harbour, where fragments of
the colossal statue of Apollo
still lie. Mount Kynthos
(really a hill, 370 feet high)
can be seen on the right.

Athenian *amphiktions,* on the lines of those at Delphi,
administered the temple.

The ruins of the sanctuary are vestigial and be-
wildering. By the House of the Naxians above the old
harbour, which was on the other side of the mole from
the existing one, are the foundations of three temples.
There is one of the sixth century, constructed of *poros*
stone; the temple of the Athenian League, begun in
477 but not finished until the third century, and a
temple of Parian marble of the fourth century.
Against the north wall of the Naxians' house stood
a grandiose statue of Apollo, carved of Naxian
marble. Its base bears a celebrated inscription in
archaic Greek of the seventh century: 'I am of the
same marble, statue and pedestal.' There is also a
fourth-century dedication 'The Naxians to Apollo',
and many graffiti of Venetian and seventeenth-
century travellers.

Apollo was represented as a *kouros* (youth), in
characteristic posture with hands on thighs. He wore
a metal belt. But he was short-lived; when Nikias
went to Delos at the head of an Athenian embassy in
417 BC, he took with him a bronze palm tree, of
which the base survives. (Apollo, it was told, was

born under a palm tree). A gust of wind knocked
the bronze against the statue, which it overthrew.
It was probably re-erected in its later position but
it became a colossal ruin, like the statue of
'Ozymandias' in Egypt, or the Colossus of Rhodes.
Its head was still on its shoulders but the trunk
was severed. The indefatigable Admiral Sir Kenelm
Digby, chief collector of marbles for king Charles I,
saw it fallen and broken in two pieces about its
slim waist. Only two fragmentary lumps now survive
of the body, having baffled Venetian attempts to
remove them. A hand is in the Delos Museum,
part of a foot is in the British Museum. Apollo
was the first pagan deity to satisfy, albeit un-
wittingly, the human craving for holy relics.

The Delians, after some shuttlecock experiences
with Athens and Sparta, only threw off Athenian
control with the advent of the Ptolemies, the kings
of Egypt so called after their founder, Alexander's
general Ptolemy. After establishing his capital at
Alexandria in Egypt, he achieved its primacy in the
Hellenistic world by hi-jacking Alexander's body on
its passage from Babylon. He also conquered
Cyprus, thereby assuring himself of the timber

necessary for the building and maintenance of a fleet, with which he dominated the Aegean.

The years from 314 to 146 BC were Delos' golden age. The island was once more the independent centre of a Confederacy. The sanctuary was enriched by offerings from all over the known world. This tiny island now became the 'common mart of all Greece' as Strabo called it. Inscriptions record the names of ninety-eight states who were, at different times, voted 'most favoured nation' treatment by the senate and people of Delos. With the foreign merchants came their gods – Isis and Sarapis among them. The Syrians had their own sanctuary, the Jews their synagogue.

By 250 BC the dusk was at hand. Roman merchants had appeared; in 166, with Roman connivance, the Delians were finally expelled from the Confederacy by the Athenians, and Delos, to counterbalance the commercial power of Rhodes, was declared a free port.

After the sack of Corinth in 146, the refugees found a new home in Delos, and now Mammon competed with Apollo. Slaves, in great demand on the *latifundia* of Italy, were one of the chief commodities. They were the principal trade of the Mediterranean pirates, until those suppliers were completely eradicated by the great Pompey in 67 BC.

In 88 BC Mithridates of Pontus attacked the island. He massacred the inhabitants and razed the city to the ground. In 69 Delos was sacked again, this time by Mithridates' allies the pirates. Its day was done. Pausanias, in his time, said that if the temple guardians were withdrawn Delos would be uninhabited – as the city is today. Philostratus, writing in the third century AD, says that the Athenians put the island up for sale. But there were no offers.

And so this most famous shrine, which had known the devotion of men for an unbroken span of two thousand years, ended by becoming an unwanted, unsaleable, plot of barren ground.

A quarry for building-stone, at the mercy of pirates, barbarians, Frankish knights, roving marble-snatchers – English, many of them – that was the fate of Delos for centuries. Only in 1873 was scientific exploration and restoration undertaken by the French. After a century, Delos shines again as one of the most precious gifts to the world of French genius.

The modern visitor finds the ruins more complex, harder to comprehend, even than those of Delphi. One of the reasons why Delos is so greatly loved is that owing to this very fact, many a pilgrim gives up the task from the start, and is content to saunter, to enjoy the incomparable views of sky and sea, to dream of days gone by, of gods and men, of poets, from Homer to Byron. He will visit the Sanctuary, and then beyond it, the avenue of the Naxian Lions, five of the original nine, made of Naxian marble. (A sixth, removed in the seventeenth century, guards the arsenal in Venice). Beyond is the clubhouse of the Beirut Poseidoniasts, with its four chapels, one dedicated to almighty Rome. To the north, beyond the Museum, lies the gymnastic quarter, stadium, palaistra and xystos, or covered track. It was on this side of the island that the Ionian pilgrims landed. It holds a wonderfully tranquil charm to-day.

From the top of Mount Kynthos, we can survey the sanctuaries of the foreign gods, and the maritime quarter, down there on the shore, with its scores of warehouses, opening on to a quay bordering one of the four basins of the commercial harbour. They seem to have but little connection with holy Delos, with no street joining them to the dwelling-places of the inhabitants. That is because the commerce of Delos was essentially a transit export-import trade.

This disjointure makes the houses and the theatre of the city all the more outstanding and appealing. Here, in this complex, we have the human, as opposed to the divine, Delos. 'Rich men, furnished with ability, living peaceably in their habitations' dwelt and prospered here. These houses belong to the Hellenistic age, the three centuries which began with Alexander and ended with Augustus.

It was for long the fashion to decry the Hellenistic age. It was regarded as 'decadent', 'derivative' – or any other opprobious epithet which came to the minds of desiccated dons who preferred to pore and quarrel rather than to live and love. Nowadays, we know the Hellenistic age for what it was – one of the most germinal epochs of ancient history, an age which produced amazingly gifted scientists, such as Eratosthenes, who calculated the circumference of the earth to within 10 per cent; Hipparchus of

Mosaic head of a leopard in the House of Dionysus in Delos. The virtuosity of the mosaic artist consisted in using the hardest possible medium, stone tesserae, to represent the softest and most delicate surfaces such as the inside of the creature's ear, or his whiskers.

Philip V, last king of Macedon and lord of the Cyclades, dedicated a magnificent Stoa, 234 feet by 36, to Apollo on Delos. He was defeated by the Romans at Cynoscephelae in 197 BC.

Nicaea, the astronomer who established the precession of the equinoxes, and Aristarchus of Samos who discovered the heliocentric nature of our universe some seventeen hundred years before Copernicus. More familiar are the names of Euclid and Archimedes. In literature and criticism (that is the ordering of the great Alexandria Library, from which we derive almost all our later classical manuscripts, at many removes) Theocritus, who was to have a deep influence on Virgil, and Callimachus, who wrote hymns to Apollo and to Delos among others, are pre-eminent.

Virgil was by no means the only, albeit the greatest, Roman to be influenced by Hellenism. Hellenistic Greece was the only Greece that all Romans knew at first hand, and therefore the Greece which influenced them and their thought – the legacy of Hellas which Rome transmitted to us. Not until the Renaissance of the fourteenth and fifteenth centuries of our era was there such an age of intellectual ferment. It is the phantoms of these latter-day Delians that we meet as we walk among their houses and in their theatre.

Pentreath knows Delos as well as anyone. Here is his description of the quarter:

'This so-called Theatre Quarter is full of interest and worth a long exploration. Some of the shops still contain what might be called heavy fixtures, vats, marble tables, olive presses, or heavy storage vessels for grain or oil. Between some of the shops a narrow passage will lead into the splendid courtyard or atrium of a rich man's house, with its columns surrounding a shallow impluvium surfaced with

The columns of the akropolis
at Lindos, Rhodes.

mosaic. These impluvia would, it seems, normally have had a few inches of rainwater in them, and this of course would well show up the mosaic design, but they are really decorative tank tops, for under all these mosaic surfaces there are deep water tanks cut into the rock. The best of the big houses are those of Dionysus, of the Trident, and beyond and above the theatre, of the Masks and of the Dolphins. The houses get their names from their mosaic floors: two are quite exceptionally fine and show Dionysus riding his tiger, and, in the House of the Masks, his panther. The design of the Roman house with its central atrium open to the sky lets in air and light and sun but keeps out cold draughts.'

It also keeps out thieves and other unwanted intruders. The best mosaics came, or at any rate the finely worked centre-piece came, from ateliers in Beirut, as is shewn by the signature of the artist on one of them, in the house of the Dolphins. The virtuosity of the mosaic-artist consisted in using the hardest available medium, that is the tessera of stone or lapis lazuli, to represent the softest natural objects, such as the feathers of a bird, or, as here, the downy inside of an animal's ear. The walls of the chambers are decorated in fresco, or imitation marble. The houses were of two storeys, and one of them is the earliest three-storey dwelling known to us. They all had drainage connected to the main street sewer system. The narrow streets were lit at night by lamps placed in niches in the walls.

The vanished life of Delos has been consigned to the lizards which scramble and dodge about its ruins, to the frogs who clamour in its forsaken cisterns, to the amazing spiders who spin their vast and delicate webs across its vacant porticoes. From a Greek anthology of the first or second century AD

Trees growing among the ruins of the theatre on the green island of Thasos.

comes this passage describing the island's sorrow at the passing of her days of glory:

'Would I were still drifting before the breath of all winds, rather than that I had been stayed to shelter homeless Leto. Then had I not so greatly mourned my poverty. Ah, woe is me: how many Greek ships sail past me, Delos the desolate, where once men worshipped. Hera is avenged on me for Leto, with vengeance late but sore.'

Delos the desolate? No, not for us. For us it is still the island of Apollo the Bright, of Artemis the Huntress, of Dionysus. . . . And so, in memory, may it always remain.

In deserted Delos it is the dead who speak: that silent island is loud with the voices of long ago. What a contrast with the other isles of Greece. They are almost all of them stridently alive. Great and small, they have one thing in common, and one only, that each is completely different from all the others. It is this quality, this utterly Greek individualness, that makes them so vital a part of contemporary Hellas.

Most Greek they are, and paradoxically Greek, as we should expect in the land which invented the word. Because of all Greek lands it is the islands on both sides of mainland Greece, which have known the longest terms of *xenokratía*, or foreign rule.

In 1204, after the rape of Constantinople by the Franks, the Aegean Islands were given by the Crusaders to Venice. (The Venetians also held Crete for four whole centuries, and Corfu from 1386 to 1797). The Venetians established twenty small fiefs in the Aegean, each dependent on the Republic. Most of them were insignificant, but there was a 'Duke of Naxos', a 'Grand Duke of Lemnos' and a 'Marquess of Cerigo' (Kythera). In 1210 Marco Sanudi, first duke of Naxos, took an oath of fealty to the Latin emperor, Henry of Flanders; and as a reward was made feudal superior of the other Aegean barons, with the grandiose and Gilbertian title of 'Duke of the Archipelago and Sovereign of the Dodecanese'. With the fall of Constantinople most of these baronies ceased to exist; but the dukes of Naxos survived for another century. So did the Knights of St John in Rhodes and Kos; they were only dislodged in 1522.

In the seventeenth century the islands were ransacked by English marble-hunters. Sir Kenelm Digby has already been mentioned. Sir Thomas Roe, ambassador to the Porte, acted for Charles I's rival, the Duke of Buckingham. Both were overreached by the Reverend William Petty, chaplain to the earl of Arundel (1580–1646), one of whose prizes was the famous Parian stone.

From 1645 to 1669, when the Turks were fighting the Venetians for Crete, the islands were alternately occupied by either side. In 1669 Crete fell to the Turks. In 1770, when war broke out between Turkey and Russia, who was now for the first time making her presence felt in the Crimea and Black Sea, the Russian fleet spent the winter at Paros and Russia annexed eighteen of the Cyclades to her empire, as vassals of which they remained for four or five years. By the treaty of Küchük Kainardji ('Little

A statue of Aphrodite from the first century BC. Archaeological Museum, Rhodes.

Teakettle') in 1774, the Turks were forced to accord to Russia a vague protectorate over Greek shipping, which was allowed to wear the Russian flag, in place of the Ottoman. This was to have a preponderant influence on the creation of a Greek national marine, which in the War of Independence would be a deciding factor. When the war broke out in 1821, the Duke of Wellington, who was no friend of any independence except that of England from France, observed that the issue would be decided by sea-power; because he, the great land general, one of the greatest of all time, knew that he had only prevailed in Spain because he was sustained by the Royal Navy. And so it came about. After the decisive battle of Navarino in 1827, many of the islands were restored to the emergent Greek kingdom. But it was only in 1947 that the Dodecanese were formally restored to the motherland.

Thasos is one of the loveliest and remotest of all Greek islands. It was colonized from Paros at the beginning of the seventh century, by command of the oracle of Delphi. The *oikistes*, or founding father, was called Telesikles, and he was later reinforced by his son the poet Archilochus. Its harbours made it a valuable trading-post, both on the east-west line of communication and on the Greece–Black Sea run. The present twin harbours are protected by moles which stand on foundations of the sixth century BC. Its picturesque acropolis was crowned with a temple of Athena, now buried beneath the ruins of a Genoese castle. A wall 4,000 yards long with ten gates protected the town; and Thasos was called a rampart of Hellenism against the northern barbarians. Polygnotus the painter came from Thasos, and so did a schoolboy prodigy called Theagenes, who at the age of nine carried off a full-size bronze statue from the agora. He went on to win no less than 1,400 prizes at the various national Games. After his death, a jealous detractor came at night to flog the bronze statue of the hero set up by his proud fellow-citizens. The statue fell and killed him, whereupon the image was cast into the sea as being a homicide. Famine followed. The Delphic oracle ordained the recall of all exiles. They were recalled: the famine continued. A second appeal produced the answer 'You have forgotten Theagenes.' The statue was hauled up by a fisherman and there was food for all. This story is worth recalling because it is typical of the childish strain in the Greek character, which could even engage the venerable oracle itself in such pranks.

The Thasos Museum has a fine *kouros* of the sixth century, carrying a ram on his shoulder, as shepherds still do in Greece and Turkey, the remote ancestor of the 'Good Shepherd' of Christian iconography.

Thasos was famous for its gold in antiquity, much of it probably brought from Mount Pangaeum on the mainland. It was to Thasos that Brutus sent the corpse of Cassius for burial after their disastrous defeat at Philippi, in 42 BC.

The Asklepieion, or healing centre, on Kos. The island was the birthplace of Hippocrates, the father of medical science.

The ancient beauty of Thasos was due to its timber, and that beauty has been preserved to our day. But here again it is to a foreigner, not to a Greek, that we owe its preservation. In 1760 Sultan Mahmoud II gave the island to the family of Mehmet Ali. It thus became, from 1813 to 1920, a quasi-independent appanage of Egypt. The reason for its still abundant forests is that it was made into a *waof*, or religious foundation in mortmain, by Mehmet Ali himself. He was born in 1769, the son of an Albanian farmer in Kavalla on the mainland, a town which still maintains a Muslim air; and Mehmet Ali's equestrian statue up on the skyline, outside his house, is the only personal Muslim memorial in all Greece. Mehmet Ali became pasha of Egypt and died at the age of eighty, after founding the dynasty which ended with king Farouk.

It is important to remember this alien intinction of the Greek scene, because otherwise we may misread the spectrum which makes up the islands' 'white radiance of eternity'. Its incidence varies greatly and subtly. In Mykonos, for instance, all is apparently modern, but for the scores of little white chapels which star the landscape. On the harbour horseshoe, with its rococo-cola ambiance, beneath the neon lights you may hear music not canned but provided by an artist playing on the *santuri*, the Greek cembalo, above which his dextrous hands flit like melodious moths. By his side are two lads dancing, not like wind-shaken reeds, but like satyrs, with much stamping, much tapping of heels, as they utter their high-pitched, plangent song. As we watch and listen the garish lights fade in the memory, and back comes Homer. We are in the hall of Antinoüs, and it is Demodocus, the divine minstrel, who is singing to us.

In Paros, only a few miles distant, an entirely new line of thought opens up. Here in the hills above the Byzantine church the famous marble quarries lie scarred and deserted; yet it was from this matrix that was brought the perfection of the human form, realized in glistening stone carved from these very hills and hauled to adorn and delight every city and temple of the known world.

Naxos, the largest of the Cyclades, seems to epitomize this spiritual mosaic quality. In antiquity its marble was much in demand for sculpture, as witness the lions of Delos. It also produced, and still produces, emery, used in the finishing of statues, and also in the carving of gems. To most modern travellers or readers, Naxos is the island were Theseus, after fleeing from Crete, abandoned Ariadne, to be rescued first by Dionysus and later by Richard Strauss. Naxos is beautiful. It captivated Byron, it captivates us. The Venetian tower is part of its history, as is the 'Latin' cathedral with its heraldic tombstones, many of them claiming pretentious titles centuries after the Duchy had fallen to the Turks.

It is in Rhodes and Kos that this harmony of contrasts is most evident. Rhodes possesses one of the most beautiful and impressive fifth century shrines at Athena still in existence. It is at Lindos, nearly 400 feet above the sea. It seems to float in the blue heaven. Yet even here are relics of the Knights

*Left*
The ruins of a marble gateway on Naxos. The island contributed the marble lions, which guarded the Sacred Lake where Apollo was born, to the island of Delos.

Hospitallers. The city of Rhodes is still inescapably dominated by them. Alongside are reminders of Byzantium, of the Turks – who still have their own quarter with its mosque – and of the Italians who in their thirty-years' occupation did all in their power to make Rhodes their show-window in the Aegean. Just outside the city is 'Mount Smith', which commemorates the English admiral Sidney Smith, who was here in 1802 to keep an eye on the French. To complete the prism, the *son et lumière* in summer. is given not only in English, French, and German, but in Swedish too.

Rhodes was famous in classical times for its sculptors, Lysippus first and most famous, then Chares of Lindos creator of the famed Colossus, a bronze statue of Helios, the sun god. Its glory, during which it was reckoned to be one of the wonders of the world, was short-lived, from about 290 BC to 225, when it was overturned by an earthquake. For eight centuries its huge fragments lay on the ground; and only in AD 653 were they collected by Saracen corsairs, taken to Tyre, and sold to Jewish merchants of Emesa (Homs) who carried them away on 900 camels to be melted down and resold. The Colossus stood, most probably, by the *mandraki* or 'sheepfold' harbour, now used as a yacht anchorage. It never spanned the harbour entrance, that fiction being merely a back-reading from Shakespeare's *Julius Caesar*, (Act I, Scene 2). Other famous Rhodian artists were Bryaxis, who carved the first cult-statue of Sarapis for Ptolemy II, and the creators of the Laocoön, Agesander, Polydorus and Athenodorus.

Even when its political fortunes were in eclipse Rhodes continued to shine. The poet Horace, who had visited it, called it 'brilliant' (*clara*). It produced a famous school of orators. Cicero studied under Poseidonius, who may rank with Aristotle as an original philosopher, and so did Julius Caesar. The Rhodians produced the earliest code of marine law, which Augustus, and later Justinian, adopted as a model. The future emperor Tiberius, the Caesar of the Gospels, spent eight years of self-imposed exile in Rhodes.

The island of Kos, too, has this double quality of ancient and almost modern (in the great hospital of the Knights at Rhodes, the rooms have both fireplaces and draught-proof ventilation). Its ancient fame rested on the fact that it was the birthplace, c. 460 BC, of Hippocrates, the greatest physician of antiquity. Its shrine of Asklepios rivals that at Epidaurus. It is renowned for a species of lettuce which, according to John Evelyn, was introduced into Europe from there. The *Coa vestis* was celebrated in Roman times for its transparency. But to-day, as in Rhodes, it is the great castle of the Order of St John which dominates the town and the harbour. Across the gulf, the Turkish shore is clearly visible. We are looking at Bodrum, the ancient Halicarnassus, birthplace of Herodotus, father of history, and the site of the Mausoleum, the tomb raised by his wife (and sister) Artemisia to Mausolous king of Caria (d. 353), whose marble head, strangely reminiscent of the Prince Consort, gazes down at us in the British Museum. In 1522 Bodrum, like Rhodes and Kos, fell to the Turks, Bodrum being the last

*Opposite*
*The Massacre of Chios* by Eugène Delacroix, painted in 1824 when the artist was twenty-six. The picture had a powerful influence in arousing pro-Greek sentiment: the Turks, in 1822, had massacred 25,000 people on the island and enslaved 47,000 others.

Another scene from the island of Thasos, the northern Aegean island noted for the cool green woods which combine with the antiquities to charm the visitor.

place in Asia Minor to be held under Christian sovereignty. About half of the inhabitants of Kos are still Muslims.

The island of Melos has been mentioned as the first home of the famous Venus de Milo. In the stone age, Melos was a source of obsidian, the sharp cutting stone which preceded the use of metals. In the sixth century BC Athens tried to coerce Melos into subjection, and when the Melians refused crushed them ruthlessly, murdering all the able-bodied males, and enslaving the women and children. Five hundred Athenians were sent to occupy this 'cemetery of Athenian honour.' The whole vile transaction has a depressingly modern ring. For English travellers the island has a curious interest. In the year 1628 Sir Kenelm Digby started writing his memoirs there. In the 1680s a party under Archbishop Gorgirenes decided to migrate to Sir Kenelm's homeland. They came to London, where they built the first Greek church in the metropolis on a site assigned them by James, Duke of York. Its memory survives in Greek Street, Soho. Near Melos is the little island of Andimilos, uninhabited, and a reserve for a rare species of chamois.

Two more off-shore islands claim our brief attention, Chios and Samos.

Chios was famous in olden times for its fertility and luxury. 'From boyhood I lived like a Chian,' says Petronius of the *Satyricon*. But it had another and more austere claim to veneration, as the birthplace of Homer. The hymn to Apollo already cited in connection with Delos contains the lines: 'Should any pilgrim ask who is the sweetest poet of all who wander here' (to Delos) 'answer with one voice, "the blind old man of Chios' rocky isle."' Thucydides supports this claim. The island contains two monasteries, one old the other modern, but each in its way a haunt of deep peace and beauty, a sermon in stone on the continuity of the spirit. In the year 1474, during the period when under Genoese control the island was once again the abode of comfort and elegance, a visitor came to study under Andreolus Giustiniani. He lodged, inevitably, in a dwelling named 'Homer's House', because it was near the so-called 'Homer's Stone'. His name was Christopher Columbus.

Chios acquired a melancholy fame in 1822, when its abortive revolt was crushed with the utmost savagery by the Turks. This inspired Eugène Delacroix to paint his famous *Massacre of Chios* (1824), which had a powerful influence in favour of Greek freedom. Delacroix was a bastard son of Talleyrand, (1754–1838), who was no friend of freedom in any form. One wonders what he thought of his son's masterpiece.

Samos is the nearest of all the islands to Asia, with which in prehistoric times it was connected, being now separated from the mainland by a channel less than a mile wide. It lies just beneath Mount Mykale, where was held the *Panionion*, or assembly of the Ionic Confederacy. The twelve cities which formed this association were Phokaea, Erythrae, Klazomenae on the Gulf of Smyrna, the city and island of Chios, Teos, Lebedos, Kolophon, Ephesus, Samos, Priene, Myos and Miletus.

Chios, traditional birthplace
of Homer. The Nea Moni, or
New Monastery, was
founded between 1042 and
1054 by the emperor
Constantine Monomachos,
'the Gladiator', who also
restored the Church of the
Holy Sepulchre in
Jerusalem. This shrine
contains beautiful mosaics.

Samos reached its greatest fame under the 'tyrant' Polycrates, in the sixth century BC. He endowed the island with what Herodotus accounted the three greatest works to be seen in any Greek land, the aqueduct constructed by Eupalinos, the mole of the harbour, and the temple of Hera, the largest known to Herodotus. It was a fitting tribute to the wife of Zeus, nasty woman though she was, whose birthplace was hard by the site. In its final form, it measured 365 feet by 179, or was to have, because it was never completed. Now, of all the grandeur, only one column still stands, and even that is incomplete. The aqueduct tunnel is over 1,000 yards long, and brought water from the source into the ancient capital. It was a marvel of surveying, for it was started from both ends and met in the middle with hardly an error. It is still possible to explore it. The mole, 400 yards long and said to be 128 feet deep to its foundations, now supports a large part of the modern Tigani, or Pithagorio, as it was officially renamed in 1955 in honour of Pythagoras, who was born in Samos, although he spent most of his life at Croton in Magna Graecia.

Among the outstanding citizens of this typically enterprising Ionian island must be mentioned Theodorus, of the mid-sixth century BC. He made a silver bowl for Croesus and an emerald seal for Polycrates himself. He was said to have invented the line, rule, lathe (the column bases of the Heraeum were turned on the lathe) and the lever. He is also credited with having introduced into Samos the art of modelling in clay and casting images in bronze and iron, that is the *cire perdue* technique already described. He and a colleague called Telecles are believed to have brought back from Egypt the canon of proportion for the human figure, such as we see it in the obviously Egyptian influenced *kouroi* of the archaic period. The most astonishing invention of this innovator was the 'damp course', for he is said by Diogenes Laertius (II.103) to have introduced a layer of charcoal into the foundations of the great temple of Artemis at Ephesus.

Byron was for once less than fair to a Greek island when he ends his great lyric with the taunt:

A land of slaves shall ne'er be mine –
Dash down yon cup of Samian wine!

Samian wine was famous, as it still is; but so was the valour of the Samians. They played a notable part in the War of Liberation. In 1832 the island received its autonomy, under the Turkish Porte, to be governed, under guarantee by the Great Powers, by a Christian prince nominated by the Sultan. This compromise constitution worked well until 1907, when the Sultan nominated a Muslim. At once Themistoklis Sophoulis a Samian who had been a lecturer in Archaeology at Athens University, headed a revolt. After five years of oppression the Muslim was assassinated, and Sophoulis, on 24 November 1912 (when Turkey was embroiled with Italy), proclaimed the union of Samos with Greece, in the shadow of a British and a French cruiser anchored in the bay. The Samians have always been practical, linking ideas and actions, like Sophoulis. It was

Aesop who started the union. He wrote his fables in Samos, but he used them to enforce points in the law courts, where he made his living.

This chapter is already overlong. It could easily be made much longer, with some mention for instance of Seriphos, the prison-island of the Roman emperors, or of Patmos, where St John the Theologian recorded the great mystical vision which we know as the Book of Revelation, in that cave, so tradition has it, below the great fortress-monastery on the height.

In all these isles, history seems to stand up clear in the incandescent light. But there is one island where it does not, an island of mystery, of almost eerie inconclusiveness. That island is Thera, the most southerly of the Cyclades, or Santorini as it used to be called, from its patron Saint Irene of Salonika, who died there in exile in 304.

So far as history is concerned, Thera exemplifies the now familiar pattern. It was populated before 2,000 BC. Its colonists founded the first European settlement in Africa, Aziris in Cyrenaica, later transferred to Cyrene itself. It had known Cretan influence, and had formed part of the Cretan thalassocracy. Since Professor Marinatos started his investigations in 1967 remarkable Cretan frescoes, of the Late Minoan period, have come to light. They are at least as fine as anything found in Knossos itself, and are now on view in the National Museum in Athens. But here arises the first mystery. If Thera was part of the Minoan kingdom, what were the artistic relations of the two? Did Thera get its art from Knossos, or was it the other way round? We do not know.

Thera became part of the Athenian empire, and was a naval base of the Ptolemies. In AD 1207 it became a fief of the Barotsi and until 1537 was included in the Duchy of Naxos.

Archaic tombs show that the ancient town of Thera was in existence before the ninth century BC. In Ptolemaic days it expanded into a considerable city of which abundant remains have been uncovered. Of interest is the Terrace of the Festivals, at the end of the highland on which the city stood, from which is visible in clear weather Mount Ida in Crete. This was the centre of the oldest Dorian cults. It is interesting to compare them with the Ionian cults, such as were celebrated at Delos. There, the long-robed Ionians were accompanied by their gracious wives. Here in Thera, the less couth Dorians delighted in the dancing – in honour of the Dorian Apollo – of naked boys, whose enthusiastic lovers recorded their admiration in graffiti on the walls. These inscriptions, dating from the seventh century BC, are not only the earliest surviving specimens of this genre of mural art, but are among the very earliest Greek inscriptions known.

All this took place on the Terrace, and on the adjoining Gymnasium of the Epheboi, in just one corner of the island. It would not in itself have bestowed very great importance on it. Yet Thera enjoys great fame, and for a very strange reason. It contains, or fails to contain, the only active volcano in Greek territory. As we sail into the great bay, we look up 800 feet. to see a white fringe of buildings atop a grey-black scree of pumice, the modern town of Thera. We cannot drop anchor here, because the sea-bed is from 700 to 1,400 feet below us. We are in fact floating in the crater of a huge volcano. The island of Nea Kameni in its middle still smokes ominously. Eruptions and earthquakes have occurred throughout the island's history. A disastrous earthquake in 1956 destroyed over half of the buildings of the little town on the cliff. The crater now covered with water is no less than twenty-nine square miles in extent. It seems to have been formed by one of the most colossal eruptions ever to take place, one which dwarfs the famous explosion of Krakatoa in 1889. Carbon tests carried out in the vast deposits of volcanic dust, both on the island and on the sea-bed, show that this convulsion occurred within a century of 1410 BC, that is just about the time that Knossos was destroyed. Here is the second mystery: did this eruption cause the downfall of the Minoan kingdom, by means of some great seismic shattering of both Thera and Crete?

Thirdly, what effect, if any, did it have on mainland Greece? Now if the great tidal wave such as eruptions on islands normally generate escaped from the vast crater of Thera, the present topographical formation of the area suggests that it would have moved north-west, that is, towards the Peloponnese, and would have cast itself onto the projection of the plain of Troezen. This is precisely where Greek folk memory holds that it did strike, for it was here, as so poignantly told in Euripides' play *Hippolytus*, that the luckless prince, fleeing from his father's jealousy and his stepmother's lust, was overcome by a great wave from the sea, a wave that bore with it a great bull, symbol of Minoan Crete. The Messenger, who had accompanied Hippolytus by the side of his chariot as he drove away into exile, thus tells the tale in the first published English verse translation, of 1781, by Robert Potter:

When we reached
The tract of desert where the shore swells high
'Gainst the Saronic Gulf, a roaring sound
Came o'er the earth, loud as the voice of Jove,
Horrid to hear . . . to the sea-beat shore we cast
Our eyes, and saw a wave so vast, it swell'd
Reaching the skies, that to our view were lost
The cliffs of Sciron, and the Isthmus now
No more appeared . . . on the high tide
It reach'd the shore close to the harness'd car;
There from its rolling and tempestuous flood
Cast forth a bull, a monster wild and vast.

The horses took fright, the chariot was wrecked, and Hippolytus was mangled and crushed, to die shortly afterwards.

Is this just an invented fable? Or is it, as so often in Hellas, a poetic embodiment of fact? We cannot tell. Thera holds her secrets, her mysteries. No wonder men have recently sought to identify the island with the lost city of Atlantis, of which Plato has told us. It is good that in our rational and inquisitive age, there should be some mysteries left, and that they should be found in Greece, and the Isles of Greece, motherland of Mysteries.

# CHAPTER IX
# Ionia—Alpha and Omega

With Chios and Samos we find ourselves not only on the threshold of Ionia, but in the Ionic Confederacy. The Ionians regarded themselves, and were regarded by others, as the fine flower of Hellenism. In *Genesis* 2. for instance, Javan (father of the sea-faring folk) bears a Semitic form of the name. To this day the Turkish word for mainland, and not only insular, Greece is Yunanistan; the Arabic is Bilad al Yunan, the Land of the Ionians.

Just who the Ionians really were is hard to determine. Homer mentions them once only (*Iliad* XIII 685) with the significant epithet *helkechitones*, long-robed, such as they are described in the Homeric Hymn to Delian Apollo. It is generally held that the Ionian Greeks were refugees from the mainland, fleeing from the invading northern Dorians as they swept down in the eleventh century BC. The claim of Athens to have been the mother of all the Ionians is, as Herodotus, himself an Ionian, declares, invalid; but Athens may well have organized the migration.

The Athenian claim is of importance, if only as shewing how outstanding the Ionians had become. What were the reasons for their eminence? We cannot define them: the spirit bloweth where it listeth. One element in the Ionian character must have been racial intermixture. Herodotus says that the Greek settlers intermarried with the Carians, the indigenous inhabitants. Relations with Lydia and Persia, though seldom friendly, were always close, like those between Briton and Norman or Spaniard and Moor. It was the Lydians who invented coinage, perhaps as early as the ninth century BC. The Persians were masters of many arts but not, to both their and our loss, that of literature, so that their contribution to human advancement has almost always been underrated.

Environment must have had its share in moulding the Ionians. The plains and valleys of the Asian seaboard are far more fertile, far more ample than any in mainland Greece. But here once again we are faced with a Greek paradox. Why was it that Ionia the rich, Ionia the spacious, provided so many of the colonies which Greeks planted during the seventh and sixth centuries BC? Miletus alone is credited with sixty and more in the Black Sea region. It can

hardly have been land hunger which prompted these enterprises, as it so often was in the case of other Greeks of both mainland and islands. Was it trade? Or simply inquisitiveness? The latter seems the truer explanation, mixed not seldom, as with the English pioneers of America, with the desire to escape from political oppression. It was their mental passion for freedom, their spiritual enterprise, that first made the Ionians famous. They were the first philosophers in the pure sense of the word.

The Ionians, as their architecture abundantly proves, were a people of almost feminine sensitivity. They were not content to accept the old hoary myths as to the origins of heaven and earth. They boldly asked questions, and as boldly suggested answers. The first of them whom we know by name is Thales of Miletus who lived in the early sixth century. He is recorded to have foretold the eclipse of the sun in 584 BC. This may not seem to us so very remarkable a feat; but an eclipse was regarded with superstitious awe even by the emancipated Athenians, and it was that very phenomenon that delayed the evacuation of the Athenian forces from Syracuse in 413 BC and thus led to their utter destruction. Thales was a practical man. He tried to unite the Ionian cities in a confederation to oppose Persian aggression. He was accounted one of the Seven Sages. (The other six were Solon of Athens, Bias of Priene, Chilo of Sparta, Cleobulos of Rhodes, Periander of Corinth and Pittacus of Mitylene).

Thales was said to have ascertained the height of the great Pyramid by measuring its shadow, cast when the shadow of a vertical rod was equal to its height. He was shrewd: foreseeing a bumper olive-crop, he made a corner in all the available olive-presses, which he later, when his prescience was justified, hired out at a large profit. Thales sought to establish unity not only politically but in the realm of physics. The whole cosmos, surely, must possess an inherent unity? For this Thales postulated water as the basic universal element. Thus it was in Ionia, in Miletus, that philosophical reflection had its birth. That was the paramount Greek invention.

The word 'philosopher' is commonplace in modern discourse, but the first actual use of the word

*philosophos* is due to Pythagoras. Pythagoras was born in Samos a generation after Thales, in or about the year 531 BC. He left the island, perhaps to escape from the tyranny of Polykrates, and as already related settled at Croton in south Italy. He held that only God was wise, and that his own humble status could only be that of a 'lover of wisdom', i.e. philosophos. Where Pythagoras excelled was not merely in applied mathematics and in music but in his insistence that philosophy should act as a practical guide to the good life. For him and his followers the spiritual regime was as strict as that of Christian monks. They took their meals in common, they practised abstinence and the examination of conscience. Because of this religious and mystical attitude to life Pythagoras soon acquired a legendary fame. His cult became associated with that of the purely mythical Orpheus. It had an abiding influence, not only on Plato but, revived as Neopythagoreanism in the first century BC, was popular at Rome and Alexandria and was eventually merged in Neoplatonism. Pythagoras therefore ranks among the most influential religious leaders of man.

Anaximandros, another Milesian and a disciple of Thales, was the first Greek to write a treatise in prose. He rejected Thales' notion that water was the original element. For him it was the 'Infinite' which he postulated as the 'Divine' surrounding and governing the innumerable worlds. He revolutionized astronomy by regarding the world no longer as hemispherical but as spherical. In the centre is the unsupported earth, shaped like a truncated column, round which circle stars moon and sun. He introduced the first sundial into Greece from Babylonia which he used to determine the equinoxes, and he drew the first map.

Anamimenes, again from Miletus and successor of Anaximander, proposed that the primal substance was a kind of air or mist. He came to be regarded as the culminating genius of the Milesian school; and later Ionian materialists looked up to him, including Demokritos of Abdera, who in the following century developed an atomic theory.

Xenophanes of Colophon near Miletus left Ionia at the age of twenty-five, probably on the Persian conquest of 545. He too migrated to the west, made observations of marine fossils at Malta and Syracuse, and gave the correct explanation of them. He is the first Greek to have insisted that the old stories about the gods would not do: they behaved, he claimed, like the basest of mortal kind. For Xenophanes there was but one supreme God, 'not like mortals either in body or mind . . . He is all sight and all mind and all hearing . . . he remains in one place, not moving at all . . . It is not seemly that he should be now here and now there . . . And he sways all things without effort, by his thought'.

Finally mention must be made of Herakleitos of Ephesus, who flourished about 500 BC. He was known as 'the dark', on account of his dark sayings. Following Anaximander he conceived the universe as being a conflict of opposites controlled by eternal Justice. His challenge to mankind is to learn to understand the discourse of nature. By finding the intelligible principle not only (like Anaximander) in

Artemis of Ephesus, the goddess called 'Diana of the Ephesians' in the Acts of the Apostles. Unlike the chaste Artemis of the Greeks, she is bedizened with pendant eggs and magical charms.

an eternal order, but primarily in the depths which the philosophic soul discovers within itself, he became the first *mental* philosopher. Of him Burn says: 'Herakleitos represents the last fine flowering of that Ionian civilization which had produced both Homer and the Milesian philosophers.' His 'doctrine of unity of opposites, taken up by Hegel (he explicitly says) from Herakleitos, passed by way of Hegel to Karl Marx, and is prominent in his and Lenin's philosophical writing. None of the intuitions

The Greek theatre at Miletus. Once a thriving port, like many of the great cities of Ionia, Miletus lost her importance when her harbours were choked with silt.

of the Ionians has been more influential.' Early in the twentieth century a great physicist, Max Born of Göttingen, said: 'I am now convinced that theoretical physics is actual philosophy.' The philosophers of Ionia had held just that conviction two and a half millenia earlier.

This achievement, the generation and development of philosophy, an achievement which was to alter the destiny of mankind, would alone be enough to make Ionia a goal for any discerning pilgrim or traveller. No other Greek centre would ever surpass it. Not even Athens. The first Stoic was a Semite from Cyprus; Epicurus, though of Athenian stock, was probably born in Samos, and after serving as a schoolmaster in Samos and studying at Teos and Colophon only settled permanently in Athens at the age of thirty-six. Sokrates and Plato were true Athenians; but Aristotle came from a little town called Stagira in Macedonia.

To visit the cities from which such genial light was

diffused is indeed to venerate holy places; but Ionia
is unique in that it flourished not only in one age,
as the nurse of one culture, but continued to enrich
civilization for more than the millenium of
Byzantium or Venice, though never like them to
dominate it. Even when Ionia was the vassal of Persia
her identity survived. Aspasia, the cultivated mistress and counsellor of Perikles, came from Miletus.
So did Hippodamus, the father of town-planning
who redesigned the Piraeus. The advent of
Alexander saw the humbling of Persia and a re-
surgence of Ionia. Later still the Attalid rulers of
Pergamum produced yet another flowering. Finally,

imperial Rome bequeathed to Ionia some of her most
splendid surviving monuments. In this brief chron-
icle it will only be possible to mention some few of
the great cities. Miletus must come first, with its
neighbouring oracle-shrine of Didyma; then moving
north Priene, Ephesus, Sardis and Pergamum.

Of all the cities of Ionia Miletus today extends the
most endearing welcome. It is not yet converted, like
Pergamum or Ephesus into an 'attraction', caged
in wire and pock-marked with booths and kiosks.
Rambling among these unspoilt ruins, in this remote
and tranquil countryside, where the poppies blaze
amid the corn and the sheep wander over the meagre

sward, it is hard to realize that we are treading the very ground of that great and prosperous city of old. Like so many other cities of ancient Asia, it has lost its harbours. There were four, from which Milesian colonists carried her arts, her philosophers and her commerce to lands as far distant as Italy, Egypt and the Crimea. Minoans, Mycenaeans, Carians followed each other into the fertile promontory. A Milesian contingent fought by Priam's side at Troy. Then came the Attic immigrants who made Miletus the most famous of all the twelve communities of Ionia.

Much of the great city may still be contemplated by the modern pilgrim: the theatre built by the Greeks, and adapted like so many others by the Romans for their barbarous exhibitions of carnage; the agoras, the council-house, the stadium, Roman baths, the Byzantine tower and the ramparts and river-bed encircling the stately town planned by Hippodamus himself. Musing in this silent city on a spring day, when the white-plumed egrets wheel above the golden-hued iris which enamels the grey ruins, it is easy to recall that never-ending quest in which so many took part, from Thales to Paul the Apostle, in this very town.

Temples there were in Miletus, to Apollo, to Athena, to Egyptian Sarapis; but they were part of the scene, gentle and restorative, as temples should be. What a contrast is Didyma, twenty miles away to the south. This vast shrine too is dedicated to Apollo, but how utterly different is it from Delos or Delphi. The sanctuary was in the care of an hereditary priesthood, the Branchidae, and very well they did by it. Offerings were attracted from Persia and from Egypt.

After many vicissitudes in about the year 330 BC the Milesians began the building of a new temple of marble. It was to be on the most grandiose scale. The area covered was only a little less than that of the temple of Artemis of the Ephesians, about twice that of the Parthenon. The temple was never finished. Its great Ionic columns, two rows of twenty-one on each side, and two rows of ten at each end, with twelve more grouped in the great porch, each one almost twice as high as those of the Parthenon, must have been designed to dominate and crush. Three of them still stand. The impression made by such blatant and aggressive magnificence is disturbing. Can this Apollo really be the bright and gentle god of Delos, the sagacious counsellor of Delphi? It is hard to believe it. The precinct seems to be haunted by some more sinister, more rapacious deity. Perhaps that is why to this day, in the little shop by the gateway, one of the chief souvenirs offered for sale is a charm to avert the baneful eye of the Evil One.

At Priene, on the other side of the Meander, we are back in Milesian peace. The town we visit lies beneath a beetling acropolis, yet stands high on its terrace above the valley, where the sluggish stream threads its serpentine way to Miletus and the sea. The very name 'Meander' has added a word to the English language, so winding is its casual and ever-changing course.

We are standing in a beautiful Hellenistic town. Its streets are beautifully planned, in Hippodamian order. When Alexander the Great passed through Priene, in his triumphal and liberating march to Issus (333), he was so taken with its layout that he decided to adopt it for his own cities, most notably Alexandria, his Egyptian capital. This plan became the accepted model for grand cities. It was taken by the Spaniards to Mexico, and so became the norm for every great city on the American continent, including New York. It returned to the Old World to bestow on Europe one of its most splendid habitations, the city of Valetta in Malta, built by those same knights as had ruled Rhodes, Kos and Halicarnassus.

It is easy in Priene to imagine the daily life of those who dwelt there. There is the base of the temple, the square council-house, and a theatre with a raised stage whose origin has baffled explanation. But this theatre must have seen a very strange assembly when in the winter of 32–1 BC Mark Antony, instead of prosecuting the wars of Rome in the East, assembled all the actors and actresses he could collect for a frolic in Samos, and then assigned Priene as their place of residence. It is to be presumed that the auditorium and the dressing-rooms rang with harsher sounds than applause as the rival troupes competed in this little theatre. All is quiet now, and in spring the walls of the theatre are bright with a beautiful purple campanula which hangs from their interstices. Priene is, in fact, one of the most alluring expositions to survive of *la douceur de vivre* as lived in the Hellenistic age. At our feet shines that famous valley, which once brought, in its navigable days, wealth and movement to Priene, with the blue mass of mountains on the distant side. As we walk down the hill among the flowers to the plane trees in the village below, the storks who chatter on the roof-tops above their never-failing fountain seem to speak to us of distant lands and other

The east front of the temple of Artemis in Sardis, seen from the south. Sardis was the seat of the last Lydian kings, of whome Croesus was the most famous. It was in Sardis that coinage was invented.

times, which yet are part of our own lives. In its echoes we hear

> The moanings of the homeless sea,
> The sound of streams that swift or slow
> Draw down Aeonian hills, and sow
> The dust of continents to be.

Tennyson could turn even soil-erosion into poetry.

From this sleepy land of streams we move north again to Ephesus. What a tribute to the many-sided, prismatic life of the Hellenistic and Roman ages – this contrast between tranquil Miletus, gentle Priene and rowdy, bawdy, flamboyant Ephesus! Even now, that contrast is felt by anyone who visits Ephesus after being in the other two; for because of its interest as a site, the Turkish government have built a splendid new deepwater quay at Kuşadasi (Bird Island) and connected it to Ephesus by an excellent road, so that a busy *banlieu* has grown up, where, as of old, merchants chaffer, and where, as of old, one of their chief lines of merchandise is representations of a fertility deity, no longer Artemis (Diana), but a more primitive godlet.

'Great is Diana of the Ephesians!', cried out the mob in the first recorded trade union riot, that of the silversmiths who accused Paul the Apostle of threatening their livelihood. (*Acts* xix).

Artemis was one of the prime factors which elevated Ephesus to its proud status of 'the first and greatest metropolis of Asia'. Her shrine not only attracted rich offerings from far and wide, but its sanctity provided security for treasure or money placed on deposit there, an asset of even greater importance in that pre-credit age than it would be now. It also provided asylum, a privilege which not even the emperor Tiberius could abrogate, and many a rogue found refuge there. A second advantage to Ephesus was its site. In those days, like so many other cities now inland, it stood on the coast, at the

mouth of the river Cayster. It was the natural outlet for the trade from the Euphrates and the east, and from the righ Meander valley itself. Its history begins with the arrival of the Ionian colonists from Athens about 1100 BC. Croesus, last king of Lydia (560–540), destroyed the first Greek city, and had it rebuilt close to the shrine; but the city of which we now behold the vestiges was built by Lysimachus, the general and successor of Alexander the Great. He encircled his new town with walls which we can still see.

Ephesus flourished as never before: it became richer every day, Strabo says, through its commerce with east and west. It reached its apogee under Roman imperial rule, of which it is one of the most eloquent creations. In the nineteenth century when republics were much in fashion, it was customary to deplore the disappearance of the Roman republic Nowadays we take a saner view. The basic flaw in all republics is that they never produce enough upper classes to go round; with the result that cads and tycoons reap their ungodly harvest. That was the case in Athens, and in Rome, too. The provinces of

Pergamum, the great, steeply-raked theatre and part of the ancient city immediately below. In the distance is Bergama, the modern town.

the republic, and specially opulent Asia, were re-
peatedly reduced to desolation and penury by the
depredations of the *publicani*, the tax-farming syndi-
cates, and the rapacity of governors like the notorious
Verres unmasked by Cicero. With the advent of the
empire the whole situation changed. The tax-
farmers were controlled, and honest governors were
sent to promote the welfare of the provinces, men
such as Pliny, the friend of Trajan, even the future
emperor Antoninus Pius himself. To this golden age
Ephesus bears testimony which becomes more
abundant every year, as the Austrian excavations
proceed.

Of the great temple nothing now remains. It was
one of the wonders of the world. Its area was
approximately two-thirds of that of St Peter's in
Rome. Its roof was supported by 127 columns, with
finely carved bases. The temple was razed by Gothic
marauders, and all trace of it was lost until late in the
nineteenth century. The ruins of pre-Roman
Ephesus are buried beneath twenty feet of alluvial
soil, and this explains not only the 'late' aspect of
the buildings we now behold, but also the huge

water-logged hollow which is all there is now to
be seen of the site of the Artemisium. It was a
British railway engineer, J. T. Wood working on the
building of the Smyrna line, who in 1869 started
trenching for the ruins of the great shrine. At first
he commuted from Smyrna, fifty miles away, but
later he moved to a house nearer his work, which he
supervised clad in a frock-coat and stove-pipe hat.
He had much to put up with – the site was water-
logged, he broke his collar-bone, his workmen were
rebellious, mice ate his 'squeezes', (impressions of
inscriptions), he was nearly assassinated, the saws
he used to cut the marble froze in the blocks of stone.
But Wood liked the picturesqueness of it all. When
a British man-of-war arrived to take his finds to
London, he entertained the officers. They played
whist and hunted the wild boar.

At the end of six years, his health and his funds
well-nigh exhausted, Wood did come upon the ruins
of the Hellenistic temple. He had dug down twenty-
five feet to uncover an area 300 × 500 feet. His chief
reward was a series of sculptured column-drums
from a double row at each end of the temple. It

The ruins of the portico of the temple of Apollo at Didyma. The remains of the columns still convey a feeling of oppressive weight and size.

took fifteen men fifteen days to extract one. Several of these columns were the gifts of kings, one being inscribed 'the gift of Croesus'. They were loaded on to a ship of the Royal Navy, piped aboard as such distinguished guests deserved. When they reached London, it took twenty dray horses to get them to the British Museum.

Poor Wood! Little did he know that his excavations had stopped short of a fabulous foundation-deposit which was found, with the aid of steam pumps, by D. G. Hogarth thirty years later–many hundreds of gold or electrum objects with statues of Artemis in bronze and ivory.

Ephesus was not the titular capital of the province of Asia (which was Pergamum) but it was its chief city and the residence of the proconsul. As we walk along its great marble-paved streets, we can contemplate its theatre where the riot took place: it held 24,000 spectators. We pass baths, grand houses–one of six storeys, a library, a temple dedicated to the emperor Hadrian the great philhellene, an ornamental fountain, the Town Hall, an Odeum of almost Renaissance intimacy and charm.

In Ephesus it is easier than in any other Greco-Roman city to appreciate the variety, the comfort and the gaiety bestowed by what Pliny called 'the infinite majesty of the Roman Peace'.

This peace was no fiction: it was a grand reality; and those who lived under it have left us their testimony. To cite but one, a Greek orator and philosopher who had been educated at Pergamum, Aelius Aristides by name, who visited Rome in or about the year AD 143 in the reign of Antoninus Pius, Hadrian's successor. He delivered a panegyric on Rome.

Rome, he says, rules the world. It is the centre of every activity. 'Egypt, Sicily and the civilised part of Africa are your farms. . . . What the Atlantic means to you, the Mediterranean meant to the Persians.' And what was sovereignty in the days of the Persians? 'It was a contest to slaughter as many people, to expel as many families and villages, and to break as many oaths as possible.' How different is Rome: better even than the Greek republics of old– 'for the Athenians and the rest of the Greeks were good at resisting aggression, and defeating the Persians and spending their revenue for the public good and putting up with hardship, but they had no training in government in which they proved failures'. In this enormous empire–so much larger than any earlier one–which stretches from Ethiopia to the Black Sea, and from the Euphrates to Britain 'neither seas nor lands between are bars to citizenship, and Asia is treated exactly the same as Europe. In your empire every avenue of advancement is open to everyone'. In fine, 'to praise the empire properly would need the whole life of the empire, and that is eternity'.

Such were the feelings of an Ionian in the golden age of the Roman empire; and it is those same emotions that flood in on us as we walk the streets of their cities.

The interest of Sardis is unique. For one thing it was never like the other cities we have discussed, a maritime city. It lies sixty-five miles east of Smyrna. It is now being excavated by a well-equipped American expedition, and already much of its ancient grandeur has been revealed and restored. Its uniqueness lies in the fact that it was a Hellenistic-Roman city like many others, but unlike most, it has other equally important associations with oriental cultures. It was the capital of the Lydian dynasty which invented coinage, it was the seat of their last king, Croesus. Most significant of all for us, when the Persians under Cyrus in 547 defeated poor Croesus, Sardis became the western focus of their vast empire, and the terminus of the great Royal Road which linked Persia with the Mediterranean. The main avenue of Sardis, now partially excavated, is the Roman successor to part of this very road. In other respects Sardis follows a familiar pattern of habitation: Mycenean links are followed by Lydian relics.

After the Persian domination, Alexander the Great is here in 334, and his Seleucid successors make it a great city once again. The kings of Pergamum take it over in 180, and bequeath it with the rest of their patrimony to Rome in 133. It was one of the earliest Christian churches in Asia, one of the seven to whom the *Revelation* is addressed from Patmos, but with little for their comfort: 'I know thy works, that thou hast a name that thou livest, and art dead. Be watchful and strengthen the things which remain, that are ready to die: for I have not found thy works perfect before God.' The rebuke is mysterious, all the more so when the neighbouring churches of Ephesus and Thiatyra are commended for their steadfastness. So was Pergamum. Leaving the ever-growing vestiges of Greco-Roman Sardis, the stadium, the theatre, the temple of Artemis and the synagogue, with those Lydian and Persian undertones still standing in our ears, let us approach Pergamum itself, the last goal of our Ionian perambulation.

If Ephesus displays the most complete picture of life in the Greco-Roman world, it is Pergamum which greets us with the grandest. One thousand feet above the Caicus valley that proud citadel rears its lordly head. Its origin is not Greek, but it is not very ancient either. It was only in 282 BC that the city came into being, and in no decent way. Alexander's successor Lysimachus, the re-founder of Ephesus, committed his treasure, some 9,000 talents, say 5m sterling, to a rogue called Philetairos, for safe-keeping in his hill-fortress. Philetairos, whose name means 'loyal', changed sides and went over to Seleucus of Antioch, who gratefully 'recognized' him as dynast of Pergamum. The loyal traitor put Seleucus' head on his coins. He was a skilled manipulator. He won his neighbours with gold, he terrified his foes with steel. He started the systematic exploitation of his country's natural resources which was to be the hallmark of all his successors' work. His nephew Eumenes I succeeded him, to be followed in 241 by Eumenes' nephew Attalus I. Attalus trounced the Galatians, to whom he refused to pay the hitherto customary 'tribute'. His victory is commemorated by the famous 'Dying Gaul' statue, now in the Museo Capitolino in Rome, wrongly but splendidly immortalized by Byron as the gladiator 'butcher'd to make a Roman holiday'. Attalus co-operated with Rome, and raised Pergamum almost to the status of a great power, certainly the paramount realm in Asia. He was a notable patron of literature and the arts, and conspicuously happy in his marriage with Apollonis of Cyzicus. In 197 Attalus was succeeded by his eldest son Eumenes II, and it is to him that we owe the grandeur of the Akropolis. It is a thousand feet high. How, we wonder, could men have lived there, and on so ample a scale? Where did they get their water from? The answer is that Eumenes II constructed the boldest aqueduct of all antiquity. We can still follow its course, by the traces that survive on the northern scarp. It brought a copious supply of water from the distant mountains, and this was conveyed by a siphon to the summit of the city itself. At its lowest point, this amazing construction withstood a pressure of no less than twenty atmospheres, or over 250 pounds to the square inch. Eumenes II was succeeded in 160 by his brother Attalus II, and Attalus II by his nephew, son of Eumenes II, as

The porch of the Aesklepieion, seen from the east. This was one of the great centres of healing in antiquity.

Attalus III, who was only a boy of ten at his father's death. His reign was short, because in 133 he died, leaving the whole of his patrimony to Rome. He had exploited the inevitable, for Rome would no doubt have found some laudable excuse for appropriating so tempting a prize.

The Attalids had become a byword for wealth, the latin word 'Attalicus' being applied in the sense that Rothschild or Rockefeller would be in later epochs. The famous altar of Zeus, the 'seat of Satan' of *Revelation*, is now in Berlin. To Pergamum we owe the elegant Pergamene capital, so much beloved

by the Adam brothers and other eighteenth century architects, and also parchment. The word signifies 'Pergamene'.

The Attalids had built up a magnificent library. This excited the jealousy of the Ptolemies of Egypt, who possessed the world's greatest library in Alexandria. The Ptolemies therefore put an embargo on the export of papyrus on which the 'volumina' or scrolls of ancient literature were written. The clever Pergamenes thereupon devised a method of writing not only on the under-side of animal skins, as men had done for many years, but on both, thus

The 'Dying Gaul' apostrophized by Byron, in the Capitoline Museum, Rome. The statue is in fact that of a Galatian warrior, one of those defeated by king Attalus I of Pergamum, 259–197 BC.

introducing a far more durable book mterial, and one which was capable of illumination. Eumenes II presented the city of Athens with the portico that bears his name, and Attalus II the portico of Attalus which has recently been so admirably restored by American skill and munificence.

Like the proud Attalids, it is to Athens that we must now turn. But before we do so, let us visit the Asklepieion down in the valley below the great Akropolis. As we stand on the podium of the temple of Trajan, one of the most superb temples to be erected anywhere in the Greco-Roman world, to commemorate Rome's greatest general, our gaze falls below the cataract-like auditorium of the theatre, across the fertile valley, to a secluded dell, in which are the remains of the most perfect temple of healing to survive from antiquity. Healing of the body through the spirit was its aim. As we set out for Athens, there to end this brief pilgrimage, we too may feel that we have benefited, like those of old, through refreshment of the mind and spirit, and that we shall face life with a lighter heart, a stronger arm, and a more confident step.

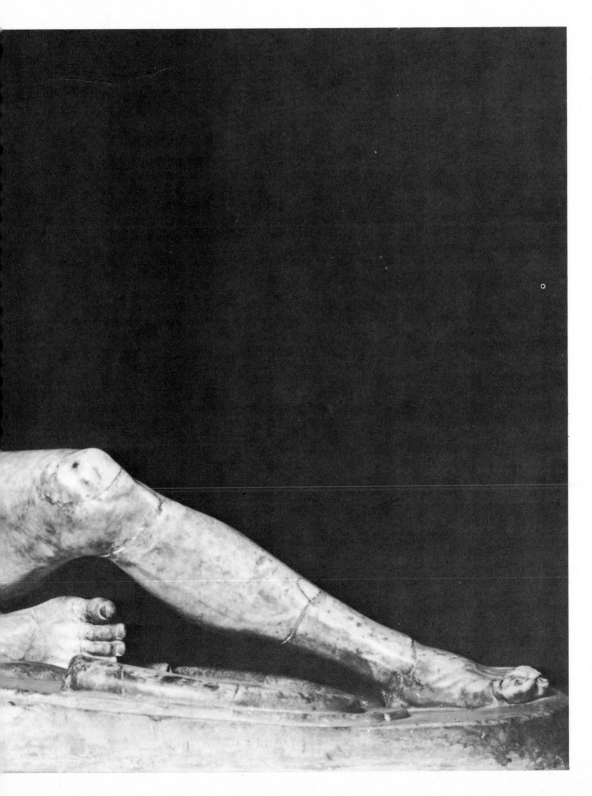

ΠΕΡΙΚΛΗΣ
ΞΑΝΘΙΠΠΟΥ
ΑΘΗΝΑΙΟΣ

# CHAPTER X
# Athens. The Violet-Crowned Citadel

'Gleaming and violet-crowned, storied bulwark of Hellas, renowned Athens, god-haunted citadel.'

'Athens, full of the glory of days gone by, yet still possessing much that is worth visiting, her citadel, her ports and the walls which link Piraeus with the city, docks constructed by great captains, statues of gods and men.'

'The town of Athens is now lying in ruins. The streets are almost deserted: nearly all the houses are without roofs. The churches are reduced to bare walls and heaps of stones and mortar . . . In this state of *modern* desolation, the grandeur of the ancient buildings which still survive here is more striking: their preservation is more wonderful. There is now scarcely any building at Athens in so perfect a state as the Temple of Theseus. The least ruined objects here are some of the Ruins themselves.'

In these three quotations may be found an epitome of the long, tragic and triumphant history of Athens. The first is the invocation from an ode of Pindar, composed in the year 476 BC to commemorate the heroic part played by Athens in the second Persian War, in which by the victories of Salamis at sea in 480 and Platea on land in the following year the imperialist aims of Persia in Europe were for ever extinguished. It was the prelude to the half century which was to witness the apogee of Athenian glory. The poem itself became famous, and was often cited by later writers. The Athenians rewarded Pindar with a handsome fee, and placed his statue among the many others of 'gods and men' in their city.

The second sentence is from the Forty-fifth Book of the history of Livy. It was written more than four hundred years later, almost a century after Athens had been humbled and looted by the Roman, Sulla, in 86 BC.

The third paragraph was written in the year 1832 by Christopher Wordsworth, soon to become headmaster of Byron's old school, Harrow. For the first time since the days of Sulla, Athens was free, after a struggle which had begun in 1821, and had cul-

minated in the battle of Navarino in 1827, a battle as decisive as that of Salamis for the fortunes of Hellas. As at Salamis, in the Greek War of Independence much more was at stake than the survival of Hellas: the issue involved the contest between reactionary tyranny on the one side and freedom of mind and spirit on the other. Freedom won, and it was on the battlefields of Greece, in the city of Athens, that once again it triumphed. But at what a cost in death and desolation. 'The least ruined objects are some of the Ruins themselves.'

Fortunately for us, that paradox is even truer now than it was in 1832. The researches and impressions of earlier travellers, such as Spon and Wheler, Carrey, Stuart and Revett, have already been mentioned, and it is easy to gather from their pages and plates what a scene of wreck and destruction Athens presented. All the more miraculous is it therefore that today we can see, not so little, but so much of Athenian grandeur.

This renaissance is due to the Athenians themselves and the reason is this: as soon as Athens became the capital of the Greek kingdom, which it did in 1834, one of the first acts of the national government was to organise an archaeological service, and the work of clearing the Akropolis was undertaken. It was gradually disencumbered of the ragged village which proliferated there under the *xenokratía*, 'foreign rule', that is Turkish domination, and what was left of the ancient monuments was once more brought to light.

The ancient Athenians once more proved their eminence. If we contemplate other focal cities (using that word in its literal meaning of hearth-place) specially Jerusalem and Rome, in conjunction with which Athens generated European civilization, we find that our observation must range over several square miles and between two and three thousand years. In Athens the whole of the architectural heritage, the title-deeds of primacy, are to be found on and beneath one hill-top of twenty-five acres; and every one of them was erected within the space of half a century. It is this which gives Athens its concentrated incandescence of spirit and delight. Stand on the Akropolis, contemplate the short span

*Opposite*
Perikles, creator of an age. A stele of the fifth century BC, now in the Vatican Museum.

127

*Above*
Part of the Parthenon frieze (south side), now in the Akropolis Museum. The ephebes rode without saddles or stirrups. The reins and bit were generally represented by appliqué bronze. See also page 34, where another section of the frieze, now in London, shows part of the procession, proceeding on foot.

of Perikles' leadership, and the surviving testimony of it in marble, and you have appropriated one of the greatest creations of human genius. Which is what its creators intended: it was designed to be, in Thucydides' famous phrase, 'a possession for ever'.

Dazzling as the prospect is, it must not mesmerize us into neglecting its ancestry. This is long and distinguished.

As early as the end of the Neolithic Age, that is about the middle of the third millenium BC, men lived on the Akropolis, and dug shallow wells on its north side. In those days, Crete was the paramount power, and Athens was tributary to her, as we learn from the legend of Theseus and Ariadne. Those first Athenians were not yet Hellenes, nor even Indo-Europeans. The Greeks called them Pelasgics.

At the end of the second millenium BC the Achaeans swept down from the north and occupied and settled in the Peloponnese. They invaded Crete and brought back with them Cretan civilization, which from its chief manifestation in Greece, namely Mycenae in the Argolid, we call Mycenaean. Vestiges of Mycenaean occupation survive on the Akropolis.

During the eleventh century BC a second wave of invaders came from the north, the Dorians. Both Minoans and Achaeans belonged to what is known as the Bronze Age, because bronze was the metal they chiefly used, for artistic, domestic and military purposes alike. Gold and silver were prized as precious metals, iron was more valuable than copper. The Dorians, using iron weapons, prevailed over the Achaeans, and so inaugurated the Iron Age in Greece.

The Athenians of later ages always claimed that they were *autochthonous*, that is sprung from the native earth, neither Achaean nor Dorian but Pelasgic. Athens, it is true, did remain inviolate when the Dorians first arrived. 'Athens alone,' in Sir Mortimer Wheeler's words, 'retained its political continuity from Mycenaean into classical times, and served as a channel for refugee-emigration to Asian Ionia'—a movement of the greatest import for mankind.

The Achaeans before their eclipse had made themselves immortal by a great enterprise, the last of many, and the only one to find its 'sacred poet', the Trojan War. In that expedition Homer tells us that among those who sent contingents was 'Athens the fair city, the folk of great-hearted Erechtheus, whom Athene daughter of Zeus reared aforetime, then settled in Athens in her rich shrine.'

Athens nevertheless was destined to feel the iron heel of the Dorians. The Akropolis fell to them, and there followed the three centuries of Greece's 'Dark Ages'. Hesiod, writing towards the end of the 8th century BC laments that he was born into 'this fifth race, this age of iron,' instead of earlier or later. One gain of this dolorous interlude was the unification of Attica, under the mythical king Theseus. That is why 'Athens', *Athenai* in Greek, is in the plural: it represents the union of several settlements. Another benefit was the birth of Athenian ceramics: the geometric-style vessels go back to this epoch.

Despite Hesiod's pessimism, the eighth century did see civilization on its feet again, and on the move as well. It was then that Greek colonization, which had been started by the Achaeans and interrupted by the Dorians was resumed. Athens' chief contribution to it was the vital patronage of the Ionian settlements, because it was from them, most notably from Miletus, that the origins of Greek philosophy were to spring. Internally, the eighth, seventh and sixth centuries were for Athens of germinal importance, both artistically and politically. The Athenian vase-painters increasingly introduced the human element into their work, thus emphasizing in clay as they would later in literature the great theme of Hellenic culture, the hegemony of man as 'the measure of all things'.

Politically, the evolution was of a structure which was to become almost stereotyped in later ages. The king gives way to an oligarchy, 'the rule of the few', whose powers were reduced by Draco in 621. In 594 Solon the Wise still further improves the lot of the ordinary citizen. Justice is assured for all, all classes are admitted to the Assembly, popular courts are created. After Solon's death these reforms are for a time frustrated by the rise of gifted individuals—tyrants; Peisistratus and his sons. The word 'tyrant' for the Greeks was something different from our use of it; it was not a description of an evil despot. Under Peisistratus Athens prospers materially, and the Akropolis is embellished, the remains of some of that early sculpture being still visible in the Akropolis Museum. Tragedy is born with Thespis in 534. In 510 the last of the tyrants is overthrown, and in 507 Cleisthenes' constitution establishes the historic Athenian Democracy, with all its faults and

all its virtues. Assaulted by the ambition of the Persians, who sacked the city in 480 BC, Athens could find the will to resist and finally repulse the invader from Asia.

The verdicts of two Greeks on Athenian Democracy may be cited. Of Perikles' pre-eminence Thucydides remarks: 'The régime was called democracy, but was in reality the rule of one man.' Pausanias, who wrote his guidebook to Greece in the first century AD, when democracy had long been dead, says of Demosthenes' suicide in 322 BC: 'Such was Demosthenes' reward for his great devotion to Athens. I heartily agree with the remark that no man who has unsparingly thrown himself into politics trusting in the loyalty of the democracy, ever met a happy death.'

Let us now ascend to the Akropolis, the high place of Periklean splendour.

How shall we approach it? Nowadays most visitors to Athens arrive by air; but in the old days only gods and goddesses or their messengers were allowed to do that. Mortals either came overland from the north, or if like us they came from overseas they landed at Piraeus, and then walked or drove up to the city between the Long Walls. These were built between 461 and 456 to connect Athens with her ports, Phaleron and Piraeus. About 455 the Phaleric wall was replaced by a third, parallel to the north or Piraeus wall. They were about four miles long and 200 yards apart. At the end of the Peloponnesian War, in 404, they were destroyed by the Spartans 'to the music of flutes' – the most harmonious act of

*Above*
Athens, a view from the 'Theseum' looking east across the Agora to the restored portico of Attalus II, king of Pergamum, 159–138 BC. The Akropolis is on the right and, on the skyline, Mount Pentelikon.

Athens benefited much from the generosity of the emperor Hadrian (opposite). He added a whole new quarter to the city, and bestowed on it a library, an aqueduct, three temples and a gymnasium. He completed the great temple of Zeus Olympios. The arch seen on the left marks the entrance to his quarter. The Akropolis is visible through it.

disarmament on record. They were later rebuilt, and were occupied by a Macedonian garrison in 322. They do not appear to have proved an obstacle to Sulla, although Livy, in the passage cited at the head of this chapter, speaks of them as still existing. Pausanias says that in his day the walls were in ruins. Only a few stones here and there remain of them.

Piraeus is now a rather grubby seaport (though possessing a fine ancient theatre and a good miniature museum), such as we read of in the works of Conrad or Genet; but in antiquity it was as splendid in its way as Athens, considered worthy of being Themistokles' burial-place. For one thing it was far better planned; Athens was so cluttered up with shrines and taboos that it was impossible to impose on it any ordered town-plan and in fact the Athenians did not really want one. They spent most of their time, as they still do, out of doors, chatting and arguing. Their houses were little more than 'pads' as they might now be termed – a fact which gave all the greater prominence to the public buildings we shall soon be surveying.

Piraeus, on the other hand, was a great commercial centre, and to promote its efficiency Perikles called in the greatest town-planner of the day, Hippodamus of Miletus, the father of the grid or chessboard pattern.

The traveller entered Athens by way of the Potter's Quarter, the Kerameikos, the name which gives us our word 'ceramic'. As he approached the city wall, he passed between monuments set up by the roadside to commemorate the dead. Many of these are still there, some raised to individuals, others to groups of warriors. It is these last which are for us the most poignant, because they remind us that it was here, on this very spot, that Perikles delivered his great funeral oration, which ranks with the Gettysburg Address as one of the great valedictories of all time. The burden of both is the same, that, as Perikles put it, 'all the world is the cemetery of great men'.

We now enter the city by the Dipylon, the Double Gate, so called because it not only opens on to the road by which we have come but is also the starting-point for the sacred road to Eleusis. We are in the Agora, the great public place of Athens – and that also is sacred. We understand why Pindar called Athens 'god-haunted', and why Perikles had to be content with planning Piraeus. But what a prospect beckons and bewitches us. There before us lies the Sacred Way, by which every fourth year the great Panathenaic procession ascended to the Akropolis, bearing a new robe for the goddess Athena. Thanks to the self-sacrificing munificence of Lord Elgin, who saved the votive sculptures from the lime-kiln, we can still relive that grand solemnity. Aloft the procession went, young men and maidens, citizens and priests, horsemen and sacrificial cattle, right onto the citadel itself.

American skill and generosity have now made it possible for us to do likewise. We enter the Agora.

Looking up at the Akropolis from the west. The Propylaea can be seen, with the little temple of Nike, (Victory), to the right

On our right is the temple of Hephaistos, for so long miscalled the Theseum. It was the shrine dedicated to the god of the metal-workers, whose forges were located in this quarter. The building has too often been dismissed as 'faultily faultless, icily regular, splendidly null'; but now that it has been restored to its proper perspective, set on its little knoll above the Agora in which we stand, we realise that it is a good example of that reticent harmony which was the Greek norm of propriety.

We note, too, how green this Agora is becoming. The reason is that its excavators decided to replant it with trees and shrubs; but only with those that flourished within its precincts in days of old – olive, pomegranate, acanthus, myrtle, oleander. We pass on; to our left, just beyond the metropolitan railway-line, was the Stoa, the famous painted porch, which gave its name to a school of philosophers. The reason is that Zeno, from Kitium in Cyprus, having arrived in Athens at the end of the fourth century BC as a penniless castaway, could not afford to hire a hall, and so held forth in the portico which had been decorated by Polygnotus from Thasos with frescoes depicting the defeat of the Persians. It was known as the Painted Portico; but is renowned to-day not for its propaganda of pride, but for its gospel of humility, of 'Stoicism'.

We press on again. It is getting warm now, and the way is steep. How glad we are to turn aside into the Portico of Attalus II of Pergamum. From the upper storey we look down on the Agora. The

*Left*
The Propylaea, the gateway to the Akropolis.

*Below*
The 'Theseum' seen from the Agora. It was a temple of Hephaistos, and became a Christian church of St George in the fourth century AD. Thus it has survived almost intact, better preserved than any other Doric temple. It is older (449 BC) than the Parthenon.

excavations allow us to behold the foundations of
many of the city's public buildings, the Stoa of
Zeus, the Temple of Apollo, the Council-chamber,
the Round-house or Municipality, the Law-court;
and right in the middle a grandiose Odeum or
Concert-hall, the donation of Agrippa the gifted
minister of the emperor Augustus.

For Athens fell under the yolk of Rome. In the
year 87, the Athenians, with that flair for backing
losers which had never deserted them, sided with
Rome's enemy, Mithridates of Pontus. Sulla, as
already recorded, sacked the city in the following
year. It never fully recovered; but we can still in
our mind's eye survey the Agora as it was both
before and after Sulla. Before, in the racy description
of Athenaeus, a third century BC author who drew
on much antique lore. Here he is, quoting a comic
poet of the fourth century BC, on the Agora: 'In
Athens you'll find everything sold together in the
same place; figs, witnesses to summonses, bunches
of grapes, turnips, pears, apples, givers of evidence,
roses, medlars, porridge, honeycombs, chick-peas,
law-suits, beestings, myrtle, allotment-machines'
(for naming juries) 'irises, lambs, water-clocks, laws,
indictments.' Even Sokrates raised his voice in the
Agora. In his Apology he says: 'If you hear me
making my defence in the same terms in which I
usually speak in the Agora, at the tables, where
many of you have heard me, and elsewhere, please
don't be surprised, and don't make a noise.'

It was the noise-making that led a later visitor to
seek the silence of the Hill of Ares, up there to the
right of the Akropolis. He had been disputing daily
in the Agora with the Epicureans and Stoics, and

had made but little headway, amid the hubbub of the market-place. His name was Paul of Tarsus. Let us follow him up the hill, and so arrive at the goal of our pilgrimage, the Akropolis of Athens.

When we consider the vicissitudes which Athens has endured, we are astounded not only by the unique beauty of what we behold but that so much of it has survived. As early as AD 267 the barbarians, Goths and Herulians, broke in by sea and land. In 435 Theodosius II ordered the destruction of pagan temples in the province of Constantinople. Athens, being in the province of Illyria, was immune from this edict but many fine sculptures, including the great statues of Athena which stood one before and the other within the Parthenon were taken to Constantinople, by that time the capital of the empire. Many temples were turned into churches, which safeguarded their existence. The Parthenon was dedicated to the Holy Wisdom, the Erechtheium to the Virgin Mother, the 'Theseum' to St George.

The general spoliation continued. By the Middle Ages, Athens was a 'deserted village'. For almost a thousand years she was to be a sleeping beauty, over whose prostrate body men of many nations would fight. In 1147 a company of Normans from Sicily occupied Piraeus. After the rape of Constantinople by the Fourth Crusade of 1204, Athens became part of the fief of Othon de la Roche, whose successor Guy was created Duke of Athens by King Louis IX, the title familiar to us from Shakespeare's *A Midsummer Night's Dream*. The Akropolis became a castle, a character it was to maintain for six hundred years. Franks, Catalans, Florentines, Venetians –

all became masters of Athens until finally it fell to the Turks after their capture of Constantinople in 1453. The Parthenon, having been originally a shrine of Athena, then an Orthodox and later a Roman Catholic cathedral, now became a mosque. The Turkish governor was installed in the Propylaea, the Erechtheium accommodating his harem.

In 1645 the Propylaea was wrecked by the explosion of gunpowder stored inside it, and in 1687, during a siege by a Venetian invader, the fatal shot was fired which blew up the Parthenon, which was being used as a powder-magazine.

Towards the end of the eighteenth century, the systematic plundering of the Akropolis began. A Frenchman, David le Roy, pioneered this shameful traffic, followed by his compatriot Choiseul-Gouffier, who in 1778 made off with a part of the frieze and two metopes recovered from the ruins. Had not Lord Elgin at great personal expense rescued as much as he did, it would be impossible for us to view as a single unit some of the greatest productions of the art of mankind. During the war of liberation in the nineteenth century the Akropolis was a battleground and further damage was done to the buildings, the Erechtheium being almost demolished.

With the establishment of the Greek kingdom the work of reconstruction, as already related, was begun. And thus it happens that after more than a century of patient work we can once again contemplate the four great masterpieces of Athenian architecture, namely the Temple of Victory, the

The Areopagus, or Hill of Ares. The summit rocks, looking east on to the Akropolis, were from the seventh century BC the meeting place of the Council of Elders and the court of justice. St Paul preached his sermon on 'an Unknown God' here in AD 51.

Propylaea, the Erechtheium and the Parthenon, in something approaching their original glory. Fortunately we have a description of them in their prime by a master hand. Plutarch, who is best known to most of us as having provided Shakespeare with the themes of three of his greatest plays, came from Chaeronea in Boeotia. He was an honorary citizen of Athens, and a priest of Apollo at Delphi. In his life of Perikles, he describes the construction of the buildings we are now looking at, which he saw at the same distance of time as separates us from our mediaeval cathedrals – he lived at the end of the first and the beginning of the second centuries AD. He starts by saying that no activity of Perikles aroused more enmity and jealousy than his public works. He was using, said his enemies, money voted for defence by the Athenians and their 'allies' for tricking the city out like a wanton woman. But Perikles knew what he was doing. His object was twofold: to immortalize the glory of Athens, and to provide full employment for its citizens.

'The materials to be used were stone, bronze, ivory, gold, ebony and cypress-wood; the skills for developing and processing them were those of the carpenter, moulder, bronze-founder, mason, dyer, worker in gold and ivory, painter, embroiderer, embosser. Then there were the contractors and suppliers of material, factors, sailors and pilots by sea, wagoners, drivers and drovers by land. Add rope-makers, weavers, cordwainers, road-builders and miners . . . The result was that practically everyone of whatever age and ability shared in the consequent distribution of the city's wealth.' Perikles the economist anticipated Keynes and Roosevelt.

Does not this glittering catalogue make us feel that we were there and saw it all going on? 'So,' Plutarch continues, 'up went the works, conspicuous in their grandeur, inimitable in the grace of their outlines . . . The speed of building was quite astonishing. People thought that each one of the buildings would take generations to finish, and yet they were all brought to completion within the heyday of a single administration . . . It is true that deftness and speed do not give a building abiding weight, nor precision of beauty; whereas time invested in painstaking creation pays off handsomely in the durability of the thing created. For this reason Perikles' works are

all the more remarkable: they were created in a short time to last for a long time. Each of them, in its beauty, was there and then an antique; but even to-day it has the flower and freshness of something newly wrought. There is a perennial bloom of youth about them, carefully preserving their appearance untouched by time, as though the unfaltering breath of an ageless spirit had been breathed into them.'

Better leave it at that. This is extrovert architecture at its apogee. Mr Osbert Lancaster's definition of architecture as the art of manipulating space is impeccable; and as a great modern architect has pointed out the space manipulated by the buildings on the Akropolis is external to them, not inside. That is why they affect us, penetrate us, as they do. The male strength of the Parthenon in its robust Doric repose, seems to smile across the plateau at the feminine, Ionic grace of the Erechtheium. The Propylaea combines both the male and the female elements in a perfect marriage, with the little Temple of Victory a posthumous child of Perikles, who died in 429, a few years before it was built.

From this eminence of time and space, we can survey all the other monuments of Athens; the Pnyx, the Areopagus, the Agora by which we came hither, the Roman market, the Library of Hadrian, the Arch which gave access to his New Town, his great Temple of Zeus (what is left of it), the Tower of the Winds – that perfect octagon, and the Clepsydra beside it, and finally the Monument of Lysicrates, the earliest surviving example of the Corinthian column used externally and the progenitor of myriads of silver table-ornaments. We can look down into the concert hall of Herodes Atticus, still used as such, and the Portico of Eumenes of Pergamum, who introduced the Roman arch into Athens in the second century BC.

Finally, we can survey the Theatre of Dionysus, the most famous in the world. As we see it now, it is a late Roman reconstruction; but it was in that very hollow that so many famous 'firsts' were presented to the world. Here Aeschylus (whose epitaph made no mention of his art, only that he fought at Marathon and gave the long-haired Persians cause for sorrow – he fought at Salamis, too) produced his Prometheus, the rebel against Heaven; here Sophokles allowed a woman to choose obedience

The Theatre of Dionysus, as reconstructed in Roman times, with a stone barrier (topped by a metal fence) to protect spectators from wild beasts exhibited in the ancient orchestra. The front seats bear the titles of the priests to whom they were allocated. The theatre probably accommodated some 17,000 spectators.

to conscience rather than to the law; here Euripides shattered every convention of hypocrisy; here Aristophanes shot folly as it flew.

Athens created all this glory in half a century, fifty years which are, forever, eternity itself.

After such a glorious noonday, any evening must seem overcast. That of Athens was. And yet the city continued to be the home of philosophy, of Plato, of Aristotle, of the Stoics and the Epicureans. Even after Sulla's brutal massacre, something of the old light still glimmered. Under the great philhellene emperor Hadrian (117–135), Athens enjoyed a tranquil sunset.

The city had known a unique continuity not only, as already noted, in time but in space as well: all dwellers in Attica of Athenian descent were citizens; and it would be unfitting to quit Athens without a visit to some at least of the country centres, say the secluded oracle-sanctuary of Amphiareion, so peaceful amid its pinewood, or the lovely seaside temple of Brauron, where Iphigeneia became a priestess of Artemis. Three of the major centres are forever famous – Sunium, Marathon and Eleusis. The cape of Sunium was to the Athenian mariner what the White Cliffs of Dover or the Statue of Liberty were to become for later navigators – the symbol of safety, the home landfall. And there on the promontory still stands the Temple of Poseidon.

Place me on Sunium's marbled steep,
  Where nothing save the waves and I
May hear our mutual murmurs sweep,
  There swan-like let me sing and die.

Byron (who carved his name on one of the columns) not only escaped death at the hands of brigands at Sunium, but went on singing for another fourteen years. From Sunium we can, like Byron, go north past the silver mines of Laurium, which supplied Themistokles with the funds to build his navy and from which the famous 'owl' coins were minted, to Marathon. When the Persians landed

there in 490 Pheidippides ran all the way to Sparta to announce the invasion, 150 miles in two days, thus becoming the prototype of all 'marathon' runners. Then came the victory under Miltiades, when in Byron's words 'Marathon became a magic name', as it has ever since remained. It was usual to bury Athenian warriors in the Kerameikos but those who fell at Marathon were laid to rest in a mound on the battlefield. It is still there. With the Athenians fought a gallant band of Plataeans. For long their sepulchre was unknown, though Pausanias mentions it. In 1971 Professor Marinatos succeeded in identifying it.

To end our tour, let us visit Eleusis. We set out from the gate by which we came in, the Double Gate, but this time we take the right-hand road, and follow the Sacred Way to the north-west. After passing the shoulder of Mount Aigaleos, crowned with the exquisite diadem of Daphni church, we descend to sea-level again, opposite 'sea-born Salamis' and so come to Eleusis, the setting for the august and secret rites of Demeter and Persephone. What these mysteries were we do not know, for those who were initiated, and there were hundreds each year for more than six centuries, were strictly bound not to reveal what they saw in that torch-lit windowless hall, of which we can still see the foundations. Emperors were proud to be adepts. Augustus himself, in Rome, once cleared the court in which he was sitting as judge, for fear that some of the evidence might compromise the sanctity of the Eleusinian rites. Prosaic Pausanias says: 'My dream forbade the description of the things within the wall of the sanctuary, and the uninitiated are of course not permitted to learn that which they are prevented from seeing.'

That the mysteries took the form of some sort of pageant, representing the external renewal of life, that much is clear. And what more fitting a close could there be to a first visit to Athens, for does not the violet-crowned city perform just that same function for the latter-day pilgrim?

The Parthenon, from the
north-east.

# Glossary

**ABACUS:** the square stone slab which is the top element of the capital of a column, on which rests the horizontal beam of the architrave.

**AGORA:** conventionally the 'market-place' or 'city-centre': here were sited the shopping and commercial facilities and the main public buildings: the accepted open space where the citizens would gather.

**AKROPOLIS:** the hill-top, fortified with walls and giving protection to the temple of the patron deity and, in early times, to the king's palace and the treasure, which was the nucleus of an early community living outside the walls but in a crisis sheltering inside them.

**AKROTERION:** the sculptured figure, tripod, disc or urn, of marble or terracotta, placed on the apex of the pediment of a Greek temple or other substantial building; sometimes also above the outer angles of the pediment triangle.

**ALTIS:** the walled enclosure of the sanctuary of Zeus at Olympia.

**AMPHICTIONY:** an association of neighbouring city-states for joint supervision of some religious institution, such as the Delphic Oracle, or the temple of Poseidon in Calauria (of equal concern to the seamen of several cities on the Saronic Gulf).

**ARCHAIC PERIOD:** from 700 BC to the end of the Persian Wars in the early fifth century BC.

**ARRIS:** the sharp edge formed, for instance, at the meeting point of two flutes in the Doric column, a vulnerable feature of the Order, rectified in the Ionic by the substitution of a flat narrow fillet between the flutes.

**ASHLAR:** applied to masonry, of squared hewn stone.

**ATRIUM:** literally, the 'place made black by the smoke' (of the altar) in a Roman house: the central feature of a Roman house, a small court open to the sky, colonnaded, four or more columns supporting the roof, and rooms opening on to the colonnade. Here stood the altar to the household gods and the death-masks of ancestors. There are many fine atria in the Roman houses of Delos, with mosaic designs on the tank-tops (impluvia) on to which fell rain through the openings above (compluvia).

**BEMA:** the rostrum of a public speaker, e.g. in the agora at Corinth.

**CELLA:** the great hall of a temple in which stood the generally colossal cult-statue of the deity.

**CENTAURS:** mythical Greek creatures, half-man, half-horse, living in Thessaly, of uncouth and libidinous habits, e.g. in the sculpture of the west pediment of the temple of Zeus at Olympia (Museum) they represent the forces of barbarism, lawlessness and uninhibited passion, despised by the Greek mind.

**CHRYSELEPHANTINE:** of a statue built up on a wooden core and covered with plates of gold – for the clothing – and of ivory – for the uncovered parts of the body. e.g. the Zeus at Olympia, and the cult-statue of Athena in the Parthenon.

**CLASSICAL PERIOD:** from the Persian Wars to the unification of Greece under Philip II and the world empire of Alexander the Great.

**CYCLOPEAN:** applied to a wall constructed, not of ashlar masonry however big the blocks, but of large boulders of a size which called for giants to handle them, and with interstices filled up with small stones. Early Mycenaean walls, at Mycenae, Tiryns, and also here and there on the Acropolis at Athens, were cyclopean.

**ENTASIS:** the slight swelling of a column so that the eye sees it as straight-sided and freed of the optical illusion which in bright light would give it the appearance of being slightly narrower half-way up its length.

**EXEDRA:** the curved marble wall, often used as a base for one or more statues, and provided with a marble bench which offered dignified and sheltered casual seating in public places.

**GEOMETRIC PERIOD:** of the post-Mycenaean period when, with the Dorian invasions, the Iron Age was fully established throughout Greece and the country had settled again after a grim period of turmoil and population movement. A sub-Mycenaean, followed by a proto-Geometric period, are transitional to the Geometric period proper, which in Athens runs from about 900 BC to 700 BC. The period is characterized by its well-shaped pottery, decorated with horizontal bands of geometric patterns, later incorporating animal and human figures.

**HELLADIC PERIOD:** applied to the Bronze Age civilization of the Greek mainland: as Cycladic refers to that of the islands, Melos and others in the Cyclades. The period corresponds roughly with that of the Minoan civilization in Crete and, like it, is sub-divided into Early, Middle and Late periods. It was during the Late Helladic period that the Mycenaean civilization developed, first at Mycenae, then at other centres in Greece and spreading throughout the Aegean.

**HELLENISTIC PERIOD**: conventionally, from Alexander the Great to the time of Augustus and the Roman Empire, i.e. 300 BC to 30 BC.

**KORE, KORAI, KOUROS, KOUROI**: conventionally applied to the clothed female and the nude male sculptured figures of the Archaic, pre-Persian War, period: they stand erect with the weight distributed between the feet, of which the left is slightly forward, but no motion is suggested; on their faces the 'archaic smile'. The best of these beautiful korai, or maidens, are in the Akropolis Museum at Athens, and of the male figures in the national Museum, where the steady progress of the sculptor's art from the purely static figure to the dynamic is readily seen and enjoyed.

**LABRYS**: a double-axe, i.e. with two blades facing right and left: a religious symbol in the Minoan period, carved on pillars and found in great numbers in miniature as votives in sanctuaries, and in more than life-size form as religious furniture.

**LABYRINTH**: double-axes (see Labrys above) were numerous as religious symbols at Knossos in the Minoan palace: the palace was a most elaborate complex of rooms, passages and staircases: hence the 'place of the double-axes' gained its second and commoner meaning.

**LAPITHS**: a mythical people in Thessaly who, under King Pirithous, fought and conquered the Centaurs. This conflict was used frequently, as in the metopes of the Parthenon, to represent the triumph of civilization over barbarism, of Greeks over Persians.

**MEGARON**: the central feature of a Mycenaean house or palace: the great room containing a large central hearth.

**METOPE**: the plain panel, alternating with the decorated cover-plate for the roof beam-ends (the triglyph) in the Doric frieze. In Classical times a sculptured relief decorated the plain space, the series of metopes round the temple illustrating a single theme, e.g. Greeks versus Amazons, Lapiths versus Centaurs, or the Labours of Herakles (as seen in the Olympia Museum).

**MINOAN**: referring to the Bronze Age civilization of Crete: Sir Arthur Evans adapted the name of the legendary King Minos of Crete to this civilization when he discovered and excavated the king's palace at Knossos.

**NEOLITHIC**: meaning 'new stone' period. EARLY from 6000 to 5000 BC; MIDDLE from 5000 to about 3000; LATE from 3000 to 2500 BC, the beginning of the BRONZE AGE.

**OBSIDIAN**: a dark glass-like mineral rock produced by volcanic action, which takes and keeps a good cutting edge: found at Melos and exported widely over the Eastern Mediterranean area: a source of wealth to Melos in neolithic times until the smelting of metals ousted obsidian for cutting purposes.

**ODEUM**: a small building in form and plan like a theatre with semicircular seating. Some were roofed. Chiefly used for musical contests and concerts and other meetings. Perikles built an odeum at Athens, the roof of which was carried on many pillars, as Plutarch says. Herodes Atticus presented a large odeum to Athens which is used, with new seating, for Greek Drama festivals to-day. CF. a beautiful odeum at Ephesus.

**ORCHESTRA**: the large circular space for the dancing of the chorus in a Greek theatre, with an altar of Dionysus in the centre: it is similar to the circular threshing-floor still seen commonly in rural Greece; for the threshing-floor, when the harvest was in and the grain stored, was the scene of the country dances and thanksgiving, the seed of Greek drama.

**PERISTYLE**: the row, or occasionally rows, of columns round a temple.

**PODIUM**: the top course of the stone foundations of a building if it projects slightly out from the line of the wall: more generally a base.

**PROPYLAEA**: the dignified entrance between columns to a sanctuary or an agora or major building within an enclosure: an idea from Minoan architecture adapted by the Mycenaeans and retained in the Classical period.

**STELE**: a stone slab set up in a public place, with an inscription recording a victory, treaty or a decree: also a grave-stone. Many beautiful funeral stelai, sculptured in relief, are to be seen in the National Museum, Athens.

**STYLOBATE**: the top surface of the stepped platform on which the line of columns stands in a Greek building.

**TEMENOS**: the enclosed area in which stood a temple.

**THEATRE**: Greek theatres were shaped like half an 'O', with the edges protruding slightly towards the stage. The Roman theatre was an adaptation of the Greek with a raised, permanent stage, and an elaborate proscenium at the back. The AMPHITHEATRE was unknown to the Greeks: it is, confusingly, a Greek name for a purely Roman structure, that is an auditorium of a complete 'O', or more usually oval, shape. The Colosseum in Rome is the largest and best-known example. The Romans often adapted Greek theatres for their bestial exhibitions.

**THOLOS**: a circular building, such as that at Epidaurus, where the circular maze-like foundations can be seen, or at Delphi, where a Doric tholos has had several fallen columns re-erected: also of the numerous underground beehive tombs of the Mycenaean period, of which the wrongly-styled 'Treasury of Atreus' at Mycenae is the best preserved and finest.

**TRIGLYPH**: a feature in the frieze of a building in the Doric Order, the three-grooved slab which alternated in the frieze with the metope: originally when buildings were wooden, a terracotta slab to protect rafter-ends from the weather. In the Classical period there was a triglyph over each column and another in each intercolumniation (space between columns). In the Propylaea the architect first dared a span wide enough for two triglyphs in the intercolumniation. This is only usual in Hellenistic times.

**TUKUL**: primitive Abyssinian hut, circular.

# Some Dates

| | |
|---|---|
| 6000–2500 BC | Neolithic Period (*see* Glossary) |
| 3000–1450 | The Minoan civilization in Crete |
| | |
| 2500–1100 | *Bronze Age* |
| 1600–1100 | Mycenaean civilization |
| *c.* 1250 | The sack of Troy by the Mycenaeans under Agamemnon |
| 1200 | Dorian invasion begins |
| 1100 | The fall of Mycenae |
| | |
| 1100– 776 | *Dark Ages* |
| | Migration of mainland Greeks to Asia Minor: Aeolians to the north, Ionians to the middle region, Dorians to the south |
| | Monarchies give way to aristocracies |
| | *Iron Age* begins |
| | Alphabet introduced into Greece |
| | |
| 776– 480 | *Archaic Period* |
| | First Olympiad in 776, the traditional date for the start of Greek history |
| | Colonization of Italy and Sicily begins |
| | |
| *c.* 750 | *The Iliad* |
| | |
| *c.* 700 | *The Odyssey.* The works of Hesiod |
| 7th century | Coinage spreads from Asia to Greece |
| 6th century | The Ionian philosophers |
| | The rise of the Persian empire |
| | Growing influence of Delphi and Olympia |
| 490– 480 | The wars with Persia |
| | The Battle of Marathon 490 |
| | Salamis 480 |
| | |
| 479– 300 | *Classical Period* |
| 431– 404 | The Peloponnesian War |

| | |
|---|---|
| 336– 323 | Alexander the Great destroys the Persian empire and founds his own |
| | |
| 300– 30 | *Hellenistic Age* |
| 241 | Carthage surrenders Sicily to Rome (founded 753) |
| 146 | Destruction of Corinth by a Roman army under Mummius |
| | Greece becomes a Roman province |
| 133 | Pergamum bequeathed to Rome by King Attalus III |
| 86 | The sack of Athens by the Romans under Sulla |
| 31 | The Battle of Actium. Augustus supreme |
| | |
| | *AD* |
| 50– 58 | St Paul in Asia Minor and Greece |
| 63 | Nero makes the first attempt to cut a canal across the Isthmus of Corinth. (Present canal begun in 1881, opened in 1893) |
| 98– 117 | Reign of Trajan |
| 117– 138 | Reign of Hadrian |
| 324 | Byzantium renamed 'New Rome' by Constantine |
| 10th and 11th centuries | Acme of Byzantine civilization. Monasteries of Daphni and Osios Loukas |
| 1204 | Fourth Crusade. The sack of Constantinople by the Latins |
| 1308 | The Ottoman Turks enter Europe |
| 1309 | The Knights of St John occupy Rhodes |
| 1453 | The Fall of Constantinople |
| 1523 | The Knights of St John leave Rhodes |
| 1821–1827 | The Greek War of Liberation. The Battle of Navarino, 20 October 1827 |
| 1912 | The Italians seize Rhodes |
| 1948 | Rhodes united to the motherland |

# Sources and Acknowledgments

Patrick Anderson *Dolphin Days* Gollancz, 1963 and E. P. Dutton & Co. Inc.
*The Smile of Apollo* Chatto & Windus, 1964

A. R. Burn *A Traveller's History of Greece* Hodder & Stoughton, 1965 and Funk & Wagnall

C. W. Ceram *Gods, Graves and Scholars* Gollancz-Sidgwick & Jackson, 1952 and Alfred A. Knopf Inc.
*A Picture History of Archaeology* Thames & Hudson, 1958 and Alfred A. Knopf Inc.

Francois Chamoux *The Civilisation of Greece* Allen & Unwin, 1965 and Simon & Schuster Inc.
J. M. Cook *The Troad*

Joan Evans *Time and Chance* Longmans, 1943 and Greenwood Press Inc.

Judith Grant *A Pillage of Art* Robert Hale, 1966 and Roy Publications Inc.

Reynold Higgins *The Archaeology of Minoan Crete* The Bodley Head, 1973 and Henry Z. Walck Inc.

Paul MacKendrick *The Greek Stones Speak* Methuen, 1963 and St Martins Press Inc.

Pausanias *Guide to Greece* (2 vols.) trans. by Peter Levi, S. J. Penguin Books, 1971

Guy Pentreath *Hellenic Traveller* Faber & Faber, 1964 and Thomas Y. Crowell Co.

Stewart Perowne *The Journeys of St Paul* Hamlyn, 1973 and World Publishing Inc.

Plutarch *Lives* trans. by John Dryden Everyman Library, J. M. Dent and Modern Library, N.Y.

Philip Sherrard *The Pursuit of Greece* John Murray, 1964 and Walker & Co.

Strabo *The Geography* trans. by H. L. Jones. Loeb Classical Library, Heinemann and Harvard University Press

Lord William Taylour *The Mycenaeans* Thames & Hudson, 1964, and Praeger Pub. Inc.

Sir Mortimer Wheeler (Ed.) *Hellenic Travellers Club Handbook* W. F. and R. K. Swan (Hellenic) Ltd, 1973

&

*Blue Guide to Greece* Ernest Benn Ltd, London

*Enciclopedia Italiana*

*Herculaneum and the Villa of the Papyri* Archaeological Guide to the Town by Amadeo Maiuri. Instituto Geografico di Agostini, Novara

*Histoire Littéraire de la Grèce* Robert Flacelière

*Oxford Classical Dictionary* Clarendon Press, Oxford

# Index